Skywater

1 9 9 0

SKYWATER

❖ ❖ ❖ ❖ ❖ ❖ ❖ ❖ ❖ ❖ ❖ ❖ ❖ ❖

Melinda Worth Popham

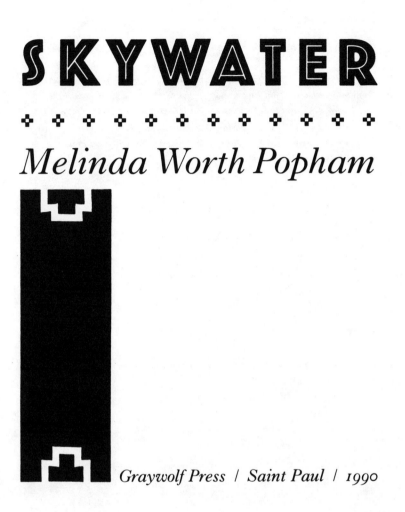

Graywolf Press / *Saint Paul* / *1990*

Publication of this volume is made possible in part by grants from the Jerome
Foundation, the National Endowment for the Arts and the Minnesota State
Arts Board. Graywolf Press is the recipient of a McKnight Foundation Award
administered by the Minnesota State Arts Board and receives generous contri-
butions from corporations, foundations, and individuals. Graywolf Press is a
member agency of United Arts, Saint Paul.

Published by Graywolf Press
2402 University Avenue
Suite 203
Saint Paul, Minnesota 55114
All rights reserved.

ISBN 1-55597-127-x

9 8 7 6 5 4 3 2
First Printing, 1990

Library of Congress Cataloging-in-Publication Data
Popham, Melinda Worth.
    Skywater / Melinda Worth Popham.
      p. cm.
    ISBN 1-55597-127-x : $17.95
    1. Coyotes—Fiction. I. Title.
PS3566.0627S58   1990
813'.54—dc20   89-77980

Author's Note

This is a work of fiction. The characters—both human and animal—are products of my imagination. However, the poisoning of groundwater by tailings from copper mines is well documented, and the methods of coyote eradication described within either have been or are currently being practiced. Concerning the coyotes themselves, the reader may assume that their behavioral phenomena are fundamentally based on fact.

Acknowledgments

I wish to thank Karen Sausman, Executive Director, and Fred Larue, Curator, of the Living Desert Reserve, Palm Desert, California, for generously sharing their knowledge of coyotes and introducing me to the reserve's resident coyotes, Sarah and Waldo. I thank Jim Coles, formerly of the Public Affairs Office, Yuma Proving Ground, U.S. Army Test and Evaluation Command, for his invaluable assistance in providing me with information concerning wildlife and military testing procedures at Yuma Proving Ground. I am solely responsible for what I made out of what they gave.

For information on the habits of coyotes and the injustices and barbarities to which they have been subjected, I am indebted to *The Voice of the Coyote* by J. Frank Dobie, *God's Dog* by Hope Ryden, *The Coyote, Defiant Songdog of the West* by François Leydet, and *Don Coyote* by Dayton O. Hyde.

Above all, I thank my husband, John H. Benton, for initiating me into his desert world and instigating our twenty-odd years of hiking, camping, and poking around the Sonoran desert. Out of it came my enthusiastic admiration for America's smallest native wolf.

M.W.P.

for William and Lillian

and, once again, John,

with love and thankfulness

The ennobling difference between one man and
another—between one animal and another—is precisely
in this, that one feels more than another.

JOHN RUSKIN,
Sesame and Lilies

I

. . . what will become of the coyote
with eyes of topaz
moving silently to his undoing. . .

RICHARD SHELTON, "Requiem for Sonora"

The old man tailboned down in the car seat and rolled the cinnamon ball over to his other cheek. The car seat, scavenged from a '52 Buick Roadmaster, was bolted onto two blocks of wood on the palm-thatched breezeway between his shack and his wife's trailer. Cellophane wrappers from many previous cinnamon balls were scattered around his feet.

Off to his left, next to the old, wooden-doored icebox where he kept his prize rocks, stood a gunnysack filled so full it stood up by itself with only some slump at the top. Every time the old man eyed the gunnysack he would switch the cinnamon ball to his other cheek, as if the thought he was turning over in his mind about the gunnysack had gotten hooked up with the rolling around of the diminishing cinnamon ball in his mouth.

The old woman stuck her head out of the trailer. She gathered herself and took a deep breath, then she saw him sitting there and softened her voice as well as whatever she had been about to shout.

"Almost sundown, Albert. Might as well get it over with," she said. "What're you doing?"

He slapped the car seat. "What's it *look* like I'm doing! Going nowhere fast, that's what."

The old man always called sitting on the bolted-down car seat "going nowhere fast." He reached into his shirt pocket, fished out a new cinnamon ball, untwisted the ends of the cellophane and popped it into his mouth. He made a point of not looking at her or the gunnysack while he did it.

The old man tipped his grizzled jaw toward the rocky outcropping midway up the mountain. "He's been there all afternoon. Watching. He knows something's up all right."

Hallie looked up at the lone coyote sitting in the shade of a paloverde tree on the outcropping: a shadow within a shadow. She had named him Brand X. "Just as well. That he's the one who'll be the first to know, I mean. He'll understand."

"Oh, he'll get the message all right," Albert said. "Loud and clear."

From his rocky outcropping midway up the mountain, the coyote named Brand X watched. Watched a red-tailed hawk slide down the steep, blue sky. Watched the drowsy jackrabbit the hawk was sliding toward. Watched a small band of javelinas trot jerkily down the dry wash. Watched another coyote, farther down the mountain, yawn then resume panting in a saguaro's slender column of shade. Watched the old man sitting on the palm-thatched breezeway at the side of his shack.

From this lookout post, Brand X held undisputed sway. It was low enough to make his ears prick at movement and sounds down below in the dry bed of the wash but high enough to lend aloofness to his scrutiny. Nothing was lost on him. The authority of his stern, golden, coyote eyes was absolute.

From this place, discovered as a pup and frequented ever since, he had made a close study of the old man and woman. That was how he knew that today something was askew.

The old man was sitting there alone, and there was a restlessness, a heaviness, a something about him that was not as always. And his place-sharer, instead of sitting with him as she always did at this time of day, was still inside the trailer, like a pocket gopher hiding in its burrow to outwait danger, poking out its head from time to time. And neither of them had done as-usual things today. The old man had done nothing with his rocks. The old woman had done nothing with her bees. And neither of them had done anything about the water tank.

But it was the full gunnysack which the old man kept glancing at that made the coyote's legs stiff with wariness and his spirit uneasy. What the coyote named Brand X feared above all else were gunnysacks.

The old woman hobbled out of the trailer. Albert gaped at her, astounded then alarmed by the sight of her. She was wearing a dress. It was white with faded red polka dots the size of silver dollars. The zipper on it went up the front from hem to collar. The dress bore the imbedded, razor-edge creases of keepsake clothing painstakingly folded and put away long ago.

Albert had not seen his wife in a dress since he couldn't remember when; and he had not seen her in *that* dress since he knew exactly when: March 23, 1944, the day the hand-delivered telegram had regretfully informed them that Peter, their only child, had been killed in the war.

It was the only dress Hallie still owned, and the only reason she had kept *it* was because she simply could not bring herself to get rid of it. The only reminders of motherhood Hallie Durham Ryder had brought with her to the desert thirty-nine years ago were a photograph album, a rubber-banded little box with all of Pete's baby teeth nested between two flat pads of cotton, and the red-polka-dotted dress.

Even more than seeing Hallie in a dress—*that* dress, hanging on her skinny, stooped body like a hand-me-down from the woman she used to be—it was the frail mortality which the dress exposed that alarmed him. The sight of her toothpick calves so thickly vined with blue veins and the skin a once-color atrophied to a ghostly, skim-milk white made her life seem to Albert all at once unbearably precious and precarious.

"What the hell!" he bellowed, as if he had been wronged.

"Oh, pipe down, Albert," she said, embarrassed, but not about to admit it, at having made him look so panic-stricken. "It's just, well, shoot, if this isn't a Wednesday I don't know what is."

They didn't keep track of the days of the week. There was no earthly reason to. What a day was called was a matter of what went on and of how it went. Albert might be having a Thursday, an ordinary day, while Hallie was having a Sunday, a special day, or a Monday, a bad day. But a Wednesday could never happen to one without involving the other. Wednesday meant catastrophe, the unspeakable coming to pass, in memory of Wednesday, March 23, 1944, the day she had been wearing the polka-dotted housedress and the telegram about Pete's death had come.

Hallie turned back into the trailer for her sunhat hanging on a nail just inside the door. Albert, afraid she would catch him at it but compelled to risk it, quickly hiked up his pant leg to take a look at his own calf. He observed that his, too, was bone-thin, ghostly white, vermicular with veins. Reassured, he stuck out his legs, crossed them at the ankle and waggled his hightopped canvas shoes up and down, as if demonstrating how capable, how lively, despite appearances, those old limbs of theirs were.

Hallie came out, pulling a warp-brimmed straw hat down hard on her head. She eyed the gunnysack as if it were a breach of faith, and the look of grim determination on her face slurred with sorrow.

"Well, let's get it over with," she said briskly. "I'll give you a hand."

"It's not the weight of it," he said, waving her off. "It's the *notion* of it."

"I know that perfectly well, Albert. I just meant that I'll come with you while you do it."

"Then do," he grunted as he dug his fists into the car seat and pushed himself up so heavily that he tottered a bit once he was on his feet.

He yanked a limp, grimy white sailor's hat off a nail and jammed it down onto his bald head which was paisleyed with brown amoeba shapes. He bunched the open top of the gunnysack and twisted and knotted it. Seizing it by the knot, he slung it over his shoulder and stepped off the breezeway into 112 degrees of arid heat. Hallie followed him, her straw-hatted head bowed low as if in reverence to the heat.

From his rocky promontory, the coyote watched them cross the distance of open ground to the water tank. Watched the crooked, stick-figure old woman with her crooked, old mesquite walking stick. Watched the bulging gunnysack as the old man swung it off his shoulder and dropped it on the ground next to the water tank. Pointing his long muzzle to the taut, blue sky, he gave voice to the uneasiness of spirit that had been gathering in his chest and throat all day.

The old man's whole body jerked as if he had been caught red-handed at wrongdoing. The old woman looked up at the rocky outcropping and saw the creamy fur of Brand X's exposed, singing throat.

"We're mighty sorry about this, old friend," Hallie said softly. "Just breaks our hearts. That's the truth. But it's not our doing. We can't help it. The water—"

"Shut up, just shut up," the old man said in a stricken voice. His gnarled fingers fumbled at the knot on the gunnysack. "Can't hear you anyway. All that hullabaloo he's making up there."

"Give it here," she said. She took the gunnysack from him and worked the knot loose. With an acknowledging grunt he took it back.

To keep tree debris from getting in the water, the low, rusty, corrugated metal tank had been situated away from the big mesquite tree. Adjacent to the water tank was a round, galvanized steel, twelve-thousand-gallon holding tank with a conical top. A pipe sticking out from the holding tank hung in midair directly above the water tank. The holding tank was connected by another pipe to a well straddled by an old, wooden-slatted windmill with a tail shaped like half of a bow-tie. The well was two hundred and fifty-two feet deep.

With the painstaking formality of a pallbearer, the formality which accompanies a mourned finality, Albert slowly circled the water tank, scattering the contents of the gunnysack into the water. The splashes they made in the quiet, dry air sounded loud, rude. When the burlap bag was empty, he held it upside down and shook it, as if grimly proving full moneysworth had been given. Then he flung the limp gunnysack onto the ground beside the tank and stomped back to the breezeway.

He rammed his beat-up, old sailor's hat down so hard onto the nail that it poked clear through. Slouching down on the car seat, he ripped the cellophane off a cinnamon ball, tossed it in his mouth, and bit right through it.

Hallie remained beside the rusty water tank, a candy-cane-shaped woman with her hands clasped over her walking stick and her head lowered in bereavement.

"That's right," she said, looking at the ground but addressing the howling coyote on the mountain. "Cry. Have yourself a good hard cry. And if I stand here any longer I'll be joining in with you."

2

*. . . and for a time I stood there thinking mostly of
the living who, buried in remote places out of the
knowledge of mankind, still are fated to share in
its tragic or grotesque miseries. In its noble strug-
gles, too—who knows?*

JOSEPH CONRAD, *Lord Jim*

As children in Manhattan, Kansas, a rhododendron hedge
had separated their yards. They themselves—Albert Ryder
and Hallie Durham—had been inseparable. Everyone but
Hallie had always called him Al. She had not only called him
Albert but, when shouting for him, had used his first and last
names. Even as an old man, it always gave him a queasy,
doomsday feeling to hear himself loudly Albert Rydered by
her, like a child called his full name by a mother who means
business.

At eighteen Albert had joined the Navy in order to see
what an ocean looked like. When he returned to landlocked
Manhattan, Kansas, it was to marry Hallie Durham, then
one year shy of graduating from the local teacher's college.
He became a house painter; she became pregnant. Upon
their only child they heaped the love they had hoped to dis-
perse among a brood. Albert privately thought that Pete being the one and only was probably due to Hallie's stubborn
streak running straight through her female parts; but he ab-
stained from saying so. Hallie privately thought the paint

fumes Albert breathed day in and day out might have affected matters; but she didn't say so.

The first boyhood summer Pete had worked for his father, Albert had proudly added him to the company name: A. Ryder & Son Painting Co. When Pete was killed in the war, Albert cancelled the order he had placed for a fourth truck for his painting crews, but he could not bring himself to paint out the "& Son" on the sides of the other three trucks.

Three months after the polka-dotted-dress day that the telegram had come, Albert sold the business—unloaded it was more like it—and announced to Hallie they were heading West. He didn't say where, just West. What he had in mind though was the Pacific Ocean.

Hallie, too grief-stricken to care one way or another about anything, gave up her job in the registrar's office at Kansas State University in Manhattan and had a garage sale. They loaded up the one remaining truck with the white elephants from the garage sale and the family heirlooms, which now had no one to inherit them, and headed not due West but on a southwestern diagonal. Along the way, they stopped at motor courts that all seemed to have a tippy swingset in knee-high weeds and a pink plaster flamingo standing on one leg in a slimy, lily-padded wading pool out front. The repetitive motor courts made Albert feel as if he had driven all day and wound up right where he had started.

Once, in Texas, they were pulled over by a state trooper suspicious of a painting truck with out-of-state plates. The matter was quickly cleared up when Albert's driver's license proved that he himself was A. Ryder, the house painter. By way of further explanation, Albert told the trooper that he was heading West because his son—Albert leaned out of the window to point to the "& Son" on the truck—had recently been killed in the war.

Hallie, tight-lipped in her bereavement, disapproved of Albert's blurting out about Pete that way. She did not want the gangly sympathy of strangers. Their mumbled, "That's a shame," or "I'm real sorry to hear it," always seemed to require her putting them at ease, like a hostess making light of a broken treasure.

When they reached the Sonoran desert of Arizona, Albert had a sudden realization—almost a revelation—that this, not the ocean coastline, was what he had had in mind when he had said "heading West." Albert had only known he wanted to live on an edge, a place where one thing stopped and another began, like an ocean meeting land. Now he had discovered that this desert, once an inland ocean, was like a dry sea within the land: a something-other-than with clear-cut limits. Then and there Albert concluded that sea and desert were two versions of the same fundamental and that he for one preferred the dryness of the one to the wetness of the other.

"Water, good old H_2O, that's what it comes down to!" he had jubilantly announced to Hallie after he had thought it all out. "Desert's desert because it ain't got enough water, and ocean's ocean on account of it's nothing *but* water. But, shoot, it's all the same difference in the end."

Hallie, while not convinced by Albert's logic, had decided that the desert was also the right place for her. It was a tiny pincushion cactus that had managed to grow from a mere hairline crack in a boulder that won her over. Its simple, wondrous bump of life hit her in a spot made acutely vulnerable by their son's recent death.

"What we're looking for, the missus and me," Albert had told the real estate man, "is something that comes as close to the center of the middle of nowhere as folks can get."

"I know just the place," the realtor said and showed them a piece of land out in the Kofa Mountains.

So it was that the proceeds from dropcloths, ladders, scaffolds, brushes, buckets, trucks, white overalls, steady employees, and a good reputation were converted into ownership of a played-out copper mine, a corrugated-tin-roof shack, dry washes and arroyos, some jagged mountains, and a good deep well. The well was what did it. That, plus, of course, the remoteness. Their land was fifty-three miles from Yuma and thirty-nine miles from the sixty-four inhabitants of Quartzsite, where the sign at Hall's Laughin' Gas Servis Station and Garage said, "Smile, you don't have to stay here but we do."

The miner's shack had two rooms. The main room was usurped by a bellicose-looking, black cast-iron stove which during most of the year was an affront to reality, but on winter nights was a blessing they counted on. Around it they squeezed in a small square eating table, two ladderback chairs, Albert's easy chair, draped with a chenille bedspread to cover the worn spots, Hallie's spring chair, and a collapsible card table for Albert's jigsaw puzzles. The other room was hogged by the four-poster, a mahogany monstrosity with hand-carved pineapples atop the posts that had been in Albert's family too long for him to want its sale on his conscience. The shack had no electricity, no running water, and no closets.

Soon after buying the land, Albert had lucked onto a MUST SELL trailer, a sleek Chrysler Airstream, for them to live in while he fixed up the shack, but he found he felt too cooped up in it to stand it even temporarily. Hallie, though, was infatuated with the trailer. It was such a shining example of a place for everything and everything in its place.

Hallie moved into the trailer; Albert stayed in the shack. They built a breezeway between the shack and the trailer and let it go at that. It reminded them of how they had begun, way back when a rhododendron bush had separated their yards. Next-door neighbors in the center of the middle of nowhere, joined by a breezeway into holy matrimony, Albert and Hallie Durham Ryder had lived in the desert that way, separately together, for thirty-nine years.

Once, a few years ago, at the Roadrunner Market in Quartzsite, Hallie had overheard Albert and herself whispered about by an enormous woman in a sleeveless, fluorescent floral shift.

"See those two old people?" she had said, poking her equally fat husband. "That's them! Those *hermits!* They been holed up out there in the Kofas since before I was even *born.* I heard they go *months* without ever coming out."

Hallie leaned hard against the dairy case. She felt as if she had had the wind knocked out of her. Tears stung her eyes. Not wanting to be caught crying, she tried hard not to blink: seventy-six-year-olds had no business bawling like two-year-olds. She could tell that Albert hadn't heard. His hearing wasn't so good anymore. Hallie Durham Ryder considered herself a good neighbor—to Albert and to the critters—and she felt part of society, the society all around her, the society of living beings in her desert neighborhood. To hear herself called a *hermit* in a tone that made it synonymous with felony or madness maligned her too profoundly, too fundamentally to let it pass.

"We are *not* hermits. We're no such thing," Hallie said, accosting the enormous woman as she stood reading bulletin-board notices out front of the pink cinderblock market, her fat-flanged arm deep in a bag of taco chips. "Homebodies, that's all we are. *Homebodies!* We like to stay put. Wouldn't hurt you any either," she said, looking the woman up and down, "to only come out for food every few months."

The woman stopped chewing and was reddening to the color of a second-degree burn as Hallie turned away.

Hallie had taken up beekeeping shortly after settling into the trailer. Her bees made cactus, mesquite, and desert wildflower honey which she sold to roadside stands and tourist shops in Yuma and Quartzsite. Albert, who had become a rockhound, sold turquoise, agates, quartz crystals, rhyolite, obsidian, chalcedony, garnets, jasper and petrified wood to rock shops and the same roadside stands and tourist shops that were Hallie's honey outlets.

Desert rocks and desert honey were popular souvenirs with the air-conditioned, visored tourists passing through what they viewed as inhuman wasteland and Biblical badlands, so Albert and Hallie made enough to make do. Neither was ambitious for more. They had had ambitions for their son, but he was dead. Nowadays, an aspiring dawn, a vaulting sunset, a packrat's treasure-filled nest, or a flash flood flaunting its wealth of water did them nicely, fulfilling their wildest dreams of riches and success. As for the rest, Hallie shrugged it off, saying, "New rockets go up. Old buildings come down. New buildings go up. Old rockets come down. Up, down, it's all the same to me."

Before discovering his true calling as a rockhound, Albert had gotten off to a false start in his new life by becoming a coyote bounty hunter. The view of coyotes which he had inherited was that they were varmints, and he believed he was doing the world a favor by helping get rid of them. Best of all, his job gave him a chance to knock around endlessly in the alien, arid, searing, armored landscape he had become so smitten with and to get to know it better—find out what went into and came out of all those mysterious holes in the ground, what left those tracks in the arroyos, and what those mineral-laden, layer-caked mountains, those geologic youngsters, were all about.

Since there was a war on, the ranchers who hired him couldn't be too choosy, even if it meant a Kansas house painter who had only hunted quail and pheasant behind bird dogs. He worked for the ranchers for a year, then for another six months he halfheartedly worked as a government trapper for the Branch of Predator and Rodent Control in the Fish and Wildlife Service. A paperweight on his boss's desk in the

Yuma office had a Mexican proverb on it that said, "God made coyotes to drive men mad." Nonetheless, between traps, strychnine-laced lard, and the cyanide guns called "coyote-getters," the government took 103,982 coyotes out of circulation in 1947, Albert's last year on the payroll.

Early on, boning up for his new job, he had looked up "coyote" in the encyclopaedia at the Yuma Public Library, and a strange thing had happened. He, a matter-of-fact, down-to-earth man who paid no attention to his dreams or any other loose talk from his psyche, had had the closest thing to a vision he was ever to experience.

After reading the brief entry on coyotes—"descended from the creodont of prehistoric times; highly adaptable predator; Mearn's desert coyote the smallest species of America's smallest native wolf; much Indian folklore about"—his eye had fallen on a small, black-and-white photograph which he took to be an illustration for the coyote entry but which was, in fact, accompanying the adjacent entry on Antoine Coypel. Even after reading the caption, "Chapel vault at Versailles by Coypel, 1709," and realizing it was the perspective and smallness of the photograph that had done it, he still could not shake the powerful illusion of the chapel vault forming the head of a primitive yet oddly realistic beast-priest coyote with the angled, clerestory windows as pointed teeth and three of the round, Baroque panels as nose and absolutely coyote eyes.

He thumbtacked it on a wall in his shack, and when Hallie asked him why, he said it was the best damn picture of a coyote he'd ever seen. Figuring it was his business if he wanted to call a church ceiling a coyote head, she had never questioned him about it again; but she did make him agree not to tear anything else out of library books.

It took him a while, but eventually Albert had gotten the hang of his job. He never did get a taste for it though. There were just too many common practices he couldn't stomach. An old-timer, in a spirit of helpfulness, would offer him a tip or a piece of advice about the most surefire way to kill pups in a den or collect coyote urine to sprinkle as lure on his traps. Albert would shake his head, toe the dirt around, and mutter, "Wouldn't work. Not with my Hallie Durham Ryder around. Thanks anyway though."

The old trappers always assumed he was referring to his wife, but Hallie Durham Ryder was also the name Albert had for his conscience. "I go home to my Hallie Durham Ryder at night," he would say.

Why Albert stopped being a government trapper had to do with a number of things: the eradication methods he drew the line at; the staggering stupidity of the sheep whose world he had been hired to make safe; his preference for puttering around the mountains with a rock hammer, a carbide lamp, and a miner's shovel; and, too, his secret admiration for his quarry, for their smarts and for what he called their born-in bone-knowing.

Sometimes he thought that coyotes knew more in their bones than he did in his head. Coyotes, for instance, knew how to scare up water by digging on the outside of a bend in the dry bed of a wash; and born-in bone-knowing was also what made them so skittish, quick to startle, and hair-triggered in their response to a world—the two-legged world Albert was part of—that wished them ill, wished, in fact, to be rid of them altogether, once and for all.

The desert rid of coyotes would be, Albert had decided, like the sky rid of stars, and, dammit, he *liked* stars, liked looking at them and just knowing they were up there, the same way he *liked* coyotes, liked hearing them, catching glimpses of them, and just knowing they were around. They belonged right where they were, coyotes and stars. They didn't ask anything of anybody, and they didn't get in the way of anything that had any business being there in the first place. Albert's former bosses, the ranchers, didn't agree, of course. And it was true that stars didn't eat and raise families and stars didn't laugh at you and play tricks on you and have ideas about how to stay alive.

Ultimately, that was what made Albert quit: this notion of extermination, of the no-more-ness of something he liked, of one variety of life getting so full of itself and deciding another variety shouldn't be on the face of the earth any more. At the end of 1947, Albert came across the Fish and Wildlife Service's summation that, between July 1, 1915—the inaugural year of the federal government's program for the systematic destruction of predatory animals—and June 30, 1947, a grand total of 1,884,897 coyotes had been exterminated. Albert wanted no part of it.

The day he found coyote scat on a trap he had set Albert laughed out loud and said at large, "You win, pal! Congratulations and best of luck!" And that was the end of that.

From the beginning, Albert and Hallie had given names to the animals they saw regularly. They talked about their comings and goings and doings the way one does of neighbors', and having names for them made it easier to talk about them. The names they first gave out had the point-blank, unsparing bluntness of schoolboys' and gangsters' nicknames: Fatso, Gimpy, Crip, Scarface, Streak, Lamebrain, Slats.

It was Hallie who hit on the idea of brand-naming them. She and Albert were forever picking up odds and ends of trash, forever tidying up the desert as if it were their own yard, and so, although begun as a kind of joke, naming the critters for the litter they found had become, for them, a system of nomenclature. Since there seemed to be no end of litter—as well as no end of new products, each bearing the manufacturer's brand name for it—she figured they would never run out of names. After rolling for miles, the dry, lacy filigree of one tumbleweed alone could collect enough trash to name a whole litter: aluminum cans, plastic cups, cigarette packs, no telling what all.

They brand-named every living creature they routinely saw, except the little ones too numerous or similar to bother with, like the lizards, the mice, the pocket gophers, the ground squirrels. The one exception was a kangaroo rat which was easily distinguishable because the fluffy plume on the tip of its tail had been bitten off in a close call with a bobcat. They named him Diet-Rite. To the rest they simply gave the catch-all name of "tin cans," because rusty, anonymous tin cans, like these little critters, were scattered everywhere around the desert.

Once they had given a brand name to a creature, no matter how casually they had slapped it on, pretty soon that name came to seem like the only right name in the world for it. To Albert and Hallie it was perfectly obvious that the spotted skunk was named Oreo, the mule deer Quaker, the cougar Cutty Sark, the mustang Nabisco, the kit fox Bisquick, the coyote Dinty Moore, the bighorn sheep Prince Albert, the javelina Colonel Sanders, the golden eagle Gallo.

Then came the springtime day, five years ago, when they first laid eyes on a coyote pup trotting alongside a javelina with two babies of her own and watched, astounded, as she stood still long enough to let all three suckle. Having brand-named generation upon generation for over three decades, Albert and Hallie Ryder felt hampered for the first time by their own naming system, stymied for a suitable name, an exceptional name, for this orphaned pup so determined to live he had convinced a javelina to mother him.

It was Hallie who thought of it, the perfect name, an anonymous name that would preserve his mystery and pay him the highest tribute their system of nomenclature could offer: Brand X.

3

When the Pleiades and the wind in the grass are no longer a part of the human spirit, a part of very flesh and bone, man becomes, as it were, a kind of cosmic outlaw, having neither the completeness and integrity of the animal nor the birthright of a true humanity.

HENRY BESTON, *The Outermost House*

There were five pups in the litter. They were three weeks old when their mother fled. Their eyes had opened, but they had never been outside their den, a shallow cave under a rocky ledge on the southern slope of a canyon.

His mother's absence finally drove the pup whom Hallie would come to name Brand X to nose warily around the entrance of the den. His hindquarters quivered with readiness to bolt back inside, but his empty belly had to know: where is she? Where is the one who takes away hunger? Where is the one whose belly we filled and who fills ours from hers?

He did not know that she had fled and would never return. Had fled because of what she had seen while out hunting food for her pups and searching for her mate, who had been missing for three days. The bond between them was affectionate and strong; this was their fourth family of pups. He was a good father. He brought food to the pups and regurgitated it for them. He stayed with them while she took her turn hunting food for herself and them.

Careworn and gnawed with worry by his absence, she had been trotting along a jeep trail when she had seen his decapitated, snarling head racing toward her on the front of a pickup truck and his bushy tail flying straight out from his nonexistent body.

A rancher had shot him, then cut off his head and mounted it, for a laugh, as a life-size hood ornament on his pickup. He had gouged out his golden eyes and replaced them with pure white shooter marbles that bulged grotesquely from the shrunken sockets. He had jammed back the lips to force the long muzzle into a crudely set snarl. As an afterthought, the rancher had also whacked off his bushy tail and attached it to the truck's antenna.

Frenzied with horror and terror at the appalling sight of her mate's severed head bearing down on her from the front of a truck, she had run under a brittlebush and bitten off her teats. Bleeding milk, she had fled to cry out her heart to the full moons of those pure white, marble eyes she had glimpsed in his head.

Seeking his mother, the pup later named Brand X ventured farther out from under the rock ledge projecting above the den's entrance. Strong light hit his new eyes for the first time, dazing him.

He whined and pawed at the place where his mother had often lain, her shape defined for him by her familiar, good smell. He licked the spot where he smelled a mouse she had eaten while lying there. Next to her shape-smell he found another's, his father's, but it was faded, less evocative.

He yipped to his brothers and sisters to come join him, to help him find the one who would take away their hunger. But they called to him to come back to them, to return to the safety of the den.

He ignored them and went still farther, following his mother's scent trails, the ones she had made coming and going from the den. Whenever he came to a crisscross of scent

trails he chose the stronger one. He had never done this before, but instinct told him what to do, told him this was the
way to find his mother. Every time he raised his head from
the scent trail the bigness of the world took him by surprise
all over again. He kept glancing back at the den to gauge his
distance from it—and to be sure it was still there.

Then one time he looked, and it wasn't there. A man was
standing in front of it, blocking it from view. His empty belly
filled with fear. He had never seen a man, but he knew with
instinctive certainty that this was a dangerous outsider. He
whined softly, thinking of his brothers and sisters within the
den, realizing he was cut off from them.

He lay down with his chin between his paws, making himself small next to a large, sandstone rock the color of himself.
He longed for the cool, twilight brown haven of the den,
longed for his brothers' and sisters' ribby, clambering,
bumptious, nestling bodies. Everything in him wanted to be
there amongst them. Everything in him warned against going there. He was three weeks old. His belly had fear instead
of food in it. He did not know what to do.

The man squatted in front of the den. He tipped his straw
Stetson back on his head and pulled a pair of heavy cotton
work gloves with cowhide fingers and palms out of the back
pocket of his jeans. He put them on, opened and closed his
hands into fists a couple of times to get them to settle right,
then picked up a length of rusty barbed wire he had set down
next to his rifle. The pickup with the coyote head bolted to
the hood belonged to him. His name was Frank Kincaid, the
same as his father and grandfather before him.

He stuck the pointed end of the wire into the den and,
working it like a feeler, probed around until it made contact
with one of the pups cowering at the back of the den. He gave
it a sharp poke to pierce the fuzzy-wooled, pink skin, then he
began to screw the barbed wire into the pup, twisting it in

until it was deep enough to give good purchase. Hand over hand, he pulled the barbed wire from the den, dragging out the pup skewered on it. The point had gone into the fold of skin between her haunch and belly and was angled toward her ribs. She writhed around on the wire and whimpered and cried, blinded by the light and the pain.

The man stood up and, setting the heel of his boot on the empty end of the length of barbed wire on which she flopped, he picked up his varmint rifle, took aim and shot her in the head. Holding down her body with his boot, he yanked the barbed wire out of her, shoved her aside and squatted down in front of the den again with the now gory length of rusty wire. It was springtime, time for spring cleaning—Frank Kincaid's annual eradication of coyote pups in their dens.

He repeated the procedure on the three remaining pups; then he leaned his rifle against a rock, coiled the barbed wire and picked up a gunnysack. The pups were heaped to one side of the entrance to the den. Three had head shots; the fourth had jerked on the impaling wire as he had fired, and the bullet had hit a neck artery, but now it was dead, too. He held up the gunnysack in one hand and tossed in the pups with the other hand, then he knotted the top. He took off the work gloves and stuffed them into a hip pocket. The fingers stuck out like a farewell wave.

Holding the rifle in one hand and the coiled wire and knotted gunnysack in the other—he usually slung it over his shoulder, but the neck-shot one would have bloodied up his shirt through the burlap—he took one last look around to be sure he had not left anything. Out of the corner of his eye, he thought he caught a flicker of movement over a ways and down from him, but he decided, no, it was just a little piece of coyote-colored rock broken off a boulder.

He worked his way down the slope to where his pickup was parked in the wash. He flung the gunnysack into the truck bed, put his rifle in the gunrack across the rear window, then stood there a minute, leaning on the open door with his elbow, taking in the wildflowers that had come into bloom: desert chicory, lupine, mallows, five-spots, poppies. He flattened out his lips and made a kissing sound and said to himself that he sure hoped that had just been a rock and not a coyote after all.

Brand X crawled on his belly to the entrance of the den. He sniffed at his brothers' and sisters' blood. He licked it tentatively. It tasted good. He smelled the smell that had come from the rifle. It made his nose recoil. So did the smell of the man. The two smells merged in his mind to make one: the stench of dangerous wrongness.

He looked down the mountainside to the wash at the bottom. What he saw down there made his bowels empty in terror. He saw his father's head jutting like a gargoyle from the front of a tan pickup truck.

It was not his mother's head, and so it had to be the other one's, the one whose eyes had spoken to him once. It had happened shortly after his own eyes had first opened. His father had been lying alone out front of the den, and his father's head, *that very head down there,* had turned, and their eyes had met—not those eyes, not those round, white stones, but his real ones, the warm, golden ones—and a heritage had been acknowledged in the look they exchanged: you are of me; yes, I am of you.

That was his father's head, but where was the *rest* of him? Where was his body? Where were his legs? Tremors of shock went through Brand X at the absolute absence, the not-thereness of his father's furred length of body, height of legs—only his head, severed at the neck on a diagonal that showed the first thrust of creamy ruff, then *nothing,* nothing more of him, nothing except the tail, his father's tail, that bushy grand banner now a lifeless trifle of fur dangling from a thin, metal rod.

Then he saw the gunnysack in the back of the truck, and again excrement spurted from him. His brothers and sisters were in that gunnysack. His brothers and sisters were with their father. That, Brand X suddenly realized, was where he, too, was supposed to be: in the gunnysack. He had been left behind, overlooked. He wanted to join them, to be reunited with them. He wanted to run to his father and brothers and sisters. But he could not run to that disembodied, snarling, white-eyed head and to that devouring, shape-changing thing that had swallowed up his brothers and sisters whole. He could not.

Brand X watched the man get into the truck, and, with the slam of the door, become a bodiless head like his father. Of his brothers and sisters nothing at all could be seen except the lumpy bulge of their combined shapes in the gunnysack.

A sudden roar came from the truck, and Brand X's father's snarling head surged forward, attached to the truck that contained his own dead pups and the man. Brand X watched and listened until its size and noise grew too small to see and hear, and all he was aware of was his terrifying aloneness in a too-big world.

He snuffled around in the sandy dirt outside the den. He found a few sun-hardened flecks of jackrabbit and mice his mother and father had eaten. He licked again at the places where the blood had been. He ate the cigarette butt the man had ground out under his boot-point, but, finding it was not food, spat it out. Until now, his mother had provided for him, but she was gone. His father and brothers and sisters were gone now, too. Everyone was gone, especially his mother. She had been his belly-filler. Now he had to find another.

He headed off downhill. He paid attention to neither the stale nor the fresh scent trails of his mother and father. They were useless to him now, those scent trails. They could have led him to a water-place, but he did not know that. All he knew was that their scent made loneliness churn with the food-longing in his belly. When at last he spotted other living beings, he veered toward them as eagerly as if they were an oasis.

The band of javelinas raised dripping snouts to eye with myopically vague menace the pup's wobbly approach to the rocky catch basin of stagnant water. Their enormous, snout-nosed heads were stuck on short, narrow, coarse-haired bodies. Their leader, bristles raised along his spine, charged him on his short, skinny, cloven-hoofed legs.

Brand X flopped onto his back and, sticking his paws into the air, pulled his tail between his hind legs, clear under to the little tassel of his penis. The javelina leader, assuaged by the pup's submissive display, swung back to the catch basin. Brand X rolled onto his belly and inched toward the water.

Sprawled lethargically on her side in the shade of a paloverde tree, a javelina sow was nursing her two babies. Her eyes were closed, and she wore a dreamy, porcine smile of contentment. The smell of her milk came to Brand X, and he changed direction: away from the insect-brothy, stagnant water and toward her. He cautiously bellied closer and closer, watching the throbbing motion of the sucklings, stalking the good smell that made him squeak with anticipation.

The sow opened her small, heavy-lashed, brown eyes and looked around, indolently accepting of whomever it might prove to be. With shortsighted eyes she dimly appraised the ingratiating upstart. The smaller of her babies grunted at the disturbance and burrowed closer against her. Being so sleepy and seeing it was, after all, just a pup, the sow gladly let her heavy head fall back onto the ground.

Brand X squirmed up to her and latched ravenously onto a spare teat. The sow's head jerked up sharply, and her hind legs twitched at the sensation of this new mouth pulling at her. Then, trusting in her leader who had sounded no alarm and being so very sleepy, she relaxed, and her milk flowed.

Brand X wriggled euphorically between his foster brother and sister as he nursed. This mother's milk did not taste like his other mother's milk. But his belly did not care.

The sow raised her head again, this time to nudge the pup's woolly flank with her snout and breathe into his fur, bestowing on him the same benediction which his first mother had: Path, little moon-caller. May you live a completed path.

4

But must I confess how I liked him,
How glad I was he had come
*   like a guest in quiet,*
*   to drink at my water-trough . . .*
And depart peaceful, pacified, and thankless?

D. H. LAWRENCE, "Snake"

Brand X loped across the loose shale of the mountain slope. Usually when he ran he felt the spread of his spirit; this time he felt only its weight. It was the same weight he felt whenever he lifted his voice to the round, white eye of his father up in the sky among the star trails. Dodging cholla cacti and chunks of sandstone fallen from the sheer vertical slabs higher up the mountain, Brand X made for the stone fish as if toward sanctuary.

Imbedded in limestone, the fossil fish was a skeletal memento of the time when the sea had covered the desert. Its imprint was perfect: the dorsal fin like a vestigial wing; the notched wedge of tail; the delicate bones feathering out from the tiny beads of vertebrae; the operculum flap; the undershot jaw; the alcove of eye.

Bushy tail pressed low against his legs, Brand X cautiously circled the fossil-bearing rock which lay in the lee of a boulder. Everything smelled and looked the intended way. No gunnysacks here. His tail wagged gently in greeting to the rock. He pawed the fish as if it were a touchstone, scraping the rough pad of his forepaw over its bony ridges and indentations, then he lifted a hind leg over it. Urine-glazed, the stone fish became still more vivid and defined. Panting softly, he sat beside the fish, sitting beside it as he had at sunset ever since he had discovered it long ago. The stony, ancestral fish was his place-sharer, his only one. Its stone bones made his spirit well up within him.

Looking down the mountain, Brand X could see the gunnysack lying in a heap beside the water tank. The sight of the brown burlap maw like that which long ago had swallowed up his little brothers and sisters and bulged with their bumpy shapes filled him with fear and queasy dread. The place where the fear was loudest was in his heart. It was pounding like a jackrabbit's that hears the snap of teeth a thorn's length behind its flying heels.

He thought about the way the old man had walked around the water tank dumping something from the gunnysack into it. Thought about how he had then thrown the sack down on the ground, throwing it down in a way that said he was glad to be done with it, throwing it down in a way that said something more than just the task itself was over and done with. Thought about the other one, the old woman, standing there looking up at him as he had given voice to his uneasiness of spirit. They were not like other two-leggeds; they were water-givers. Now they had done something dire but necessary to the water-place. Brand X understood dire necessity. Whatever they had done, he could see they, too, had an uneasiness of spirit about it.

As Brand X started down the mountain to find out what was now in the water tank, he watched the birds wheeling in raucous confusion above it. He saw the coyote named Dinty Moore sitting in a saguaro's long column of shadow farther down the slope.

Dinty Moore was always on the lookout for Brand X. Of all
the coyotes, none save Dinty Moore had persisted in seeking
him out and tailing him. The others, seeing he shunned
them, had long since given up. Small and spare like all desert
coyotes, Dinty Moore was smaller and sparer than any of the
others. Slim pickings had been Dinty Moore's daily fare for
so long that Albert said that when he howled the howls came
not from his mouth but from his belly. But no coyote had a
longer grin than he, and, skinny though he was, he hadn't
starved to death and, being eleven years old, had seen a good
many others that had.

Wagging tail held low in greeting and his roguish mouth
pulled into a submissive grin, Dinty Moore raised his muzzle
to indicate the commotion of birds above the water tank.

Brand X slackened his pace then stopped altogether. He
didn't want Dinty Moore to tag along after him. After what
had happened in the den of his first world, Brand X believed
that closeness to his own kind would end his path in a gunnysack. Beginning with the javelina, his milk mother, Brand
X had made for himself a world aloof from all other coyotes.
He wanted to keep it that way. He rounded on Dinty Moore
to quash any thought he had of following and trotted off
without a backward glance.

Spurned but ever hopeful, Dinty Moore gave Brand X the
leeway of a generous head start and headed down the mountain after him. Always guarded about anything risky or even
suspiciously out of the ordinary, he was not sorry to have to
hang back and let the gap between them widen.

Near the base of the mountain, Brand X came upon a family of kangaroo rats frolicking in the dirt near their burrow
under a brittlebush. Immune from water worries, they neither drank nor passed water, and their carefree mirth as they
leaped and tumbled doubled Brand X's gathering dread that
the only reliable, year-round water-place, the one his javelina

mother had introduced him to as a weaned pup, might have failed.

He was accustomed to water-places failing. Wild burros fouled them; thirsty beings depleted them; the sun sucked them dry. Water was fragile, vulnerable. He knew that. But he had thought the water-place of the two-leggeds could never become empty. Like the dreamed-of, yearned-for, blue vastness of Skywater itself, it had always been a miraculous exception: permanent, full, beyond the power of sun or tongue to make it dry.

Brand X dropped down into the wash. Its banks were sparsely lined with catclaw, paloverde and mesquite, and its sandy bottom was dented, pocked and wrinkled with the tracks of the many creatures who used this dry water-trail as their regular route to the water tank.

Every inch on the alert, Brand X proceeded down the middle of the wash. The complicated subtleties of desert colors in his fur were as strikingly ingenious in their camouflage as the obscuring vivacity of a tiger's stripes in the shadow of bamboo. His black-rimmed, golden eyes beneath their brows of lighter fur were intense, serious, intelligent. In deference to the uneasiness he felt about the water tank, he changed his long-standing habit of springing out of the wash from the tortoise-hump rock. He stayed down in the wash around two more small bends before he scrambled up the bank, emerging just where he had calculated to be: downwind of the water tank.

Eyes riveted on the gunnysack, he flattened himself on the ground and waited. Waited for the gunnysack to give itself away, to reveal itself, to betray what it was doing there beside the water tank. He did not mind waiting. It was of benefit to him. Waiting would help him to live a completed path. Every so often he slowly raised his head. To test the air. To look around. Down in the wash behind him he heard the *tchuk-*

tchuk of Dinty Moore's paws on the wash's sandy bottom. He had forgotten about Dinty Moore.

He saw the man and woman sitting in the breezeway as they did every day at dusk. But his hackles rose in alarm when he saw what they were looking at: the spot where he always bounded out of the wash to come to the water tank. They, too, were waiting. Not just casually waiting for him to appear at his usual exit point from the wash. No, his arrival was as eagerly awaited by them as a burrowed gopher's by a coyote's patient jaws. He was the prey of their eyes.

The birds wheeling above the water tank caught sight of Brand X and sharpened their cries as if it were his fault they couldn't swoop down for their customary evening drink.

Appraising the moment, Brand X began to stalk the gunnysack lying some fifty yards away. He flicked a glance at the old ones and saw that they now saw him. The woman was sitting forward with her elbows in her red-polka-dotted lap; the man leaning forward with his fingers splayed on his knees. The rigidity of their stillness increased his already profound apprehension.

Giving a wide berth to the palm-thatched lean-to where their old truck was parked, Brand X kept his eyes riveted on the rumpled folds of the empty gunnysack as if it were capable of disappearing down a hole or striking out at him. He ignored the water tank. The gunnysack came first. From it had come whatever was now in the water-place. He closed in on it, belly close to the ground, neck extended and low, the whole of him seeming to be slung from the points of his shoulders and pelvis.

When the gunnysack was so near that he could see the weave of the burlap fibers, Brand X rushed forward, his back hunched, the hackles standing up like quills along the ridge of it, and pounced, growling, jaws gaping, upon it. Holding it down with his forefeet, he seized it in his teeth and ripped and tore at it, jerking his head from side to side and up and down. Not until he was more than certain that beyond any doubt it had been rendered harmless did he fling it away from himself. Then, to rid himself of his revulsion at having had it in his mouth, he shook himself thoroughly and, dropping down, rubbed his muzzle, first one side then the other, on the ground. He did not know if lifeless things like stones, sticks, caves, and gunnysacks had a spirit within them or not, but if they did, then the gunnysack's had to be the most horrible of all, residing within a thing that could swallow coyote pups whole.

The gunnysack destroyed, Brand X raised his head and looked down into the round metal tank. He saw a thick crust of dried droppings floating on the water, a logjam of buoyant scat. Here and there, lopsided minarets of solidified bat droppings pierced the crust. Wherever there was a small break in the crust, seeds, small wads of fur, pieces of insect shell, and other undigested bits from the decomposed scat floated intact on the water's surface.

With ears pricked forward, his golden eyes grave and puzzled, Brand X sat back on his haunches and peered intently at the befouled water. By their shapes, sizes, and smells, he could readily identify the various sources of the droppings but knew it didn't matter. Whoever they were, they had ruined the water-place, contaminated it.

He looked over his shoulder at the old man. He had done it. Had carried the gunnysack full of scat. Had dumped it into the water-place. And she had been with him. He had seen them from his lookout perch. Had watched them do it. And yet, it was not their fault. Like coyote scat on a trap, the droppings were a message.

"That's right, old pal," Albert called out from the breezeway. "Shit! The water's turned to shit! But don't look at *me* like that. It's not our doing. No siree. It's those tailings from the copper mines around here that done it. Worked their way clear down to groundwater. Made it so it's not fit for me *or* you to drink. That load of shit in the tank there is so you'd know just why it is we can't be giving you and the other critters water any more. It's poison."

Brand X looked steadily at the old man, waiting to see if he had finished speaking.

"God Almighty that coyote's got smart eyes," Albert said. "Just look at him!"

"Comes of having to use his brain to fill his stomach," Hallie said. "And that *soul* of his, shoot, it knows things older than you and me put together."

Brand X caught the sound of her low voice and turned his attention to her.

"You want to hear it from me, too?" She spread her hands in a gesture of futility. "It's just like Albert here said. No more water. Not for drinking anyhow. So you'd best go find yourself a water hole somewhere, and even if it's got a dead burro and a couple million Jerusalem crickets rotting away in it, you'll be better off drinking it than the water that comes out of our well. Might just as well cap it for all the good it's doing us now. Far as that goes, pretty soon Albert and me may be down on all fours drinking out of a water hole right alongside you."

"Speaking of drinking..." Albert said. Taking pains not to spook Brand X, he slowly eased himself off the bolted-down car seat and slipped into the shack. He always switched from cinnamon balls to sipping-whiskey at sunset when the critters—his drinking buddies he called them—came to the tank. From now on, he would be drinking alone.

"Fact is," Hallie continued, as if taking advantage of Albert's absence to share a confidence with Brand X, "we didn't know *what* was wrong. Both of us have had the trots for months. We must've lost about as many pounds between us as you weigh altogether. Take a look at Albert for yourself when he comes back out here. His face's gotten so drawn up you'd think he was sucking on lemons all the time instead of those candy balls of his.

"I don't know, I don't know. I guess the folks where we do business must've just forgotten to tell us. Or else didn't even think to. Probably thought we'd seen all about it in the newspaper or on the television.

"But, shoot, you know Albert and me. We're just like you. We don't read the papers. Don't have radio or television. Only news we get is local news, the same news you get, reading scat and tracks, listening to you coyotes sound off about things.

"Lucky for us I happened to see the headline in the paper in the rack there at the Roadrunner Market. Otherwise, we still wouldn't know what went wrong. About the water going bad I mean."

Bending her head, she rubbed her knobby hands in slow whorls over the skirt of the red-polka-dotted dress, then smoothed it over her knees and looked up.

"Bottled water, that's what we have to drink now. And, I'll tell you, it's going to break us—our pocketbooks or our backs, one or the other. It's got this stand, and what you have to do is turn the bottle upside down and lift it—"

"And if I told her once I told her a thousand times," Albert said, bursting out of the shack, glass and bottle in hand, and plunking himself down so hard onto the car seat that sloshed whiskey asterisked his pants, "to tell me, just *tell* me, when she needed a new bottle. But no! She's so *god*damn stubborn and so *god*damn independent she thought she could do it for herself. Little bitty tweaker like her and so feeble from the trots she can hardly lift one of her gallon jars of *honey,* and she thought she could heft up one of those *five*-gallon water bottles. No wonder she got her back crippled up!"

"Now just shush, Albert. You want to scare him off? Then just keep on in that loud tone of voice. At least we *have* drinking water. Even if it is out of a bottle."

Albert slumped against the back of the car seat. Being admonished over his tone of voice had suddenly made him realize that, with the critters no longer coming around to drink from the tank, he would no longer get to listen in on what Hallie said to them. They were so in the habit of talking to each other through the critters that it was hard for Albert to imagine what they would do without them as intermediaries to triangulate their worries and concerns about one another and things in general.

Then, too, there was Hallie's voice itself, the particular way she had of addressing the critters, his drinking buddies, when they came to the tank. Its tone was one of boundless cordiality and unguarded goodheartedness. It always reminded Albert of how she had talked to their son as a baby. Not that it was babytalk. On the contrary, it was a kind, confidential voice that assumed and paid tribute to the listener's worthy intelligence, an assumption which Albert found lacking in the impatient tone she often took with him.

"Now listen here, Brand X," Hallie said in that voice Albert was going to sorely miss. "I guess I don't have to tell you that you coyotes aren't going to win any popularity contest with most folks. So if I were you, I would stick just as close by here as I could. You *know* we're not going to harm you, and there's water around here. It's just a matter of finding it. Your know-how may be a little rusty, but it'll come back to you, that born-in bone-knowing Albert's always talking about.

"But from now on you're going to have to be *double* careful. Take some lessons from Dinty Moore. That old rascal knows what's what. Or Kraft, he could teach you a thing or two. Chewing off his own leg to get free of that trap sure took the edge off *his* curiosity.

"Fact is, we're real partial to you, Brand X. Always have been. Ever since we first laid eyes on you, tagging around after that sweet old sow we called Dixie."

"Well, what're you waiting for?" Albert shouted, too heartsick to hear more. "Nothing to stick around here for. Water's not fit for man nor beast. Go spread the word. Go on! Scram!"

"Albert! Don't drive him off!"

Brand X got to his feet. With slow formality he sniffed the tattered shreds of the gunnysack he had destroyed then turned to face the two old ones. He fixed them with a piercing, mesmerizing look that encompassed the linear, cold-blooded calculation of the rattlesnake and the ethereal, three-dimensional wisdom of the eagle. Holding them fast in his golden-eyed, deliberate gaze, he squatted over the shredded gunnysack that lay beside the no-longer water-place and ceremoniously defecated on it. Then he disappeared, fading into the desert evening like smoke into fog.

5

Some mystery becomes the proud.
But to be wholly taciturn
In your reserve is not allowed.
Say something to us we can learn
By heart and when alone repeat.
Say something!

ROBERT FROST,
"Choose Something Like a Star"

Dinty Moore waited for Brand X beside the red rock water hole which he and the other coyotes had been using since the ruination of the water tank. The water hole lay in a flat boulder at the base of a cliff. During flash floods, an ephemeral but powerful waterfall hurled over the cliff and down onto the boulder, and, over eons, the cascading water had pounded the middle of the boulder into a deep catch basin. The hardened band of mineral deposits and scum around the inside of it revealed, like a bathtub ring, how brimful it had been before evaporation and thirsty beings had depleted it to its present soupy level.

Dinty Moore was confident Brand X would come soon, because the first slants of sunlight were already passing through the deepest jag in the mountain, and the sun would soon climb high enough to make the lizards rise on their tiptoes so as not to scorch their bellies on the ground. For the moment, however, the merciless thorns of the teddybear chollas looked deceptively downy in the sun's easygoing, early light, and wispy strands of mare's tail clouds floated pink in the lightening blue.

Dinty Moore had been sitting there for some time, waiting with the infinite patience of those for whom time is never stagnant and who do not measure it, who simply trust in the sun and moon to show its passage. The anticipation of catching sight of Brand X picking his way up the narrow, boulder-strewn canyon had in no way dulled him to the activities going on around him: a stink beetle lumbering across a rock, a parade of Gambel quail, a flock of bats—tiny pipistrelles the size of hummingbirds—returning to their mountainside cave.

So absorbed was he in the entrancing, vivid cornucopia of each passing moment that the sudden noise of water being lapped up caught him off guard. He spun around, startled. His jaws broke into an admiring grin. Brand X had come as quietly as a falling feather.

In order to reach the low water, Brand X had had to angle himself steeply down the slick, smooth sides of the hole, leaving only his hindquarters precariously remaining on the rim. Dinty Moore listened to Brand X's tongue lapping water, the sound amplified by the bowl's hollow depth.

When he had finished drinking, Brand X threw his weight into his hindquarters and started to slowly walk his forelegs back up the slick rock. Suddenly his paws slipped, and his body lurched, tipping him down into the bowl. Dinty Moore vicariously lurched. Brand X rocked back hard, and, with a final scramble, his forelegs gained the safety of the rim. He backed away from the edge of the catch basin and sat on the flat of the boulder. Water from his muzzle spattered dark stars onto the red rock. He ignored Dinty Moore standing below with softly wagging tail and a concerned expression on his upturned face.

Jarred by his close call, Brand X knew the time had come

to let the sun drink the remaining water in this water hole. Its steep sides were as smooth as sky. A moon-caller who fell in could never climb out, not even if he had the claws of a badger. His path would end down there in the dregs. His own almost had just now.

But where would he go from now on when his tongue hung long with thirst? The water stars dried on the rock and the sun crowned above the mountain while he considered it. Dinty Moore's lingering presence was like a subtle, additional pressure on him to find an answer.

Having seen Brand X nearly fall into the catch basin, Dinty Moore knew that neither he nor Brand X would ever risk drinking there again. By the forward set of Brand X's ears and the pensive tilt of his head as he sat gazing up at the top of the waterfall cliff, Dinty Moore knew that Brand X was thinking about water-places, about where to go next.

At the top of the cliff was a window rock, a hole eroded through sandstone, and it was the round, blue eye of sky filling the hole that provided Brand X with the answer. As he sat gazing through the eyehole in the rock, it came to him. He would go to Skywater, to the unfailing, eternal, blue water-place of Skywater, the one water-place which had endured throughout all of time.

His knowledge of Skywater was ancestral, spiritual, in his blood. It was Skywater that moon-callers' tongues panted for when the sun's fierce stare drove all living beings into slit-eyed hiding, and it was Skywater that sleeping moon-callers were racing toward when their legs twitched with dream-running. And when their sun-bleached, hollowed-out skulls and picked-clean, splintered bones lay scattered in the desert, Skywater was the place where their parched spirits finally slaked their thirst. In its blue water, their spirits could float like clouds and move like the little cousins who lived in water, the ones whose tiny bones Brand X had seen pressed into stone like paw prints in sand, the ones whose bone-tracks in stone proved that once, long ago, the burnt lands had been part of Skywater.

Skywater was where moon-callers longed to be, not as spirits later on but right then, as living beings with their spirits still inside them. Now, with the water-place of the two-leggeds contaminated and the water in the slick-rock water hole too low, Brand X was swept into the strong, in-escapable current of that deepest of all longings, to drink from the place where water was still as big, as forever, and as blue, deep and all-around as the desert sky. He would cross the sun-dazed lands until he reached Skywater's shore. How-ever far, whatever direction, where land ended Skywater be-gan. Although no living moon-caller had ever drunk its blue water, Brand X sensed it was the intended way that he go there, drink from it.

He lowered his eyes from the window rock. His gaze passed like a wing shadow over Dinty Moore. Throwing his muzzle skyward, he howled with water-longing and spirit-thirst for Skywater.

Dinty Moore stared up at Brand X with such pricked, un-blinking concentration that his own being seemed suspended, nonexistent. As a dog senses its beloved owner's impending departure without even the evidence of a suitcase, Dinty Moore knew that Brand X was leaving. He also heard what Brand X was howling for and, from it, sensed not only his departure but his destination as well.

When Brand X stopped howling and opened his eyes, he looked down at Dinty Moore as if surprised to find him still there. For the first time since his arrival at the water hole, his gaze took Dinty Moore in hard.

His eyes beat down on Dinty Moore like double suns; but it was Skywater that Dinty Moore saw in them, as if Brand X's eyes had become window rocks through which blue water showed. Despair sank its talons deep into Dinty Moore's heart. He rubbed his muzzle back and forth across a rock, as if whetting his jaws, but knew no howl from him could be eloquent enough to stop Brand X from leaving.

The thought of Brand X's departure drove Dinty Moore to desperately bite and scratch suddenly urgent itches all over himself. He frantically contorted himself this way and that, alternating legs and teeth, to reach itches behind his ears, on his belly, face, back, chest, attacking himself in a frenzied flurry of hind feet and teeth because he was helpless to prevent a hopeless journey and because, without Brand X, he would be bereft of a defining presence, a guiding spirit.

Among the coyotes, the position of honor belonged to Brand X. He was their finest example of themselves to themselves: a survivor against the odds. He was not their leader. They had no leader. He asked nothing of them, wanted nothing from them. He had taken no mate. He made his own trail. Yet the other coyotes held him in the highest esteem—and none more so than Dinty Moore—because his desire to live a completed path was so strong that, as a pup, he had made a javelina sow his water-place.

No matter how hard Dinty Moore bit and scratched himself an image of Brand X crossing the sun-dazed lands stayed snagged in his mind like a flutter of stray paper impaled on a catclaw branch. He imagined Brand X harassed and challenged by moon-callers hostile to his crossing of their home ground, his drinking from their water-places, his hunting of their prey. Imagined Brand X a starved and parched outlander, exhausted by vigilance and struggle, with no shelter whatsoever from the sun's glare, not even a spindly creosote bush.

Dinty Moore gave up his frantic scratching and biting. He looked up at Brand X sitting atop the water-hollowed, water-hallowed boulder. The outer guard hairs of his fur shone in the early sun, radiantly outlining him. The magnificence of him filled Dinty Moore's spirit, replenishing it as rains would this water hole. He knew what he must do: go with him.

6

Fare thee well;
The elements be kind to thee, and make
Thy spirits all of comfort!

SHAKESPEARE, *Antony and Cleopatra*

Brand X passed his last day on home ground in his usual way, holed up in the shade. But knowing that it was his last day to lie in the abandoned badger hole under the double-trunked paloverde made him homesick for it even while he still lay in it. He had long ago enlarged the hole to suit himself, and now its contours and its smell were uniquely his. All day long he cherished its familiarity as he never had before.

Restless with anticipation, he spent the day slipping in and out of sleep, rousing, stretching, yawning, resettling himself, dozing. The soporific calls of mourning doves and the tinkly-jingle of cactus wrens lulled him to sleep. Flies, gnats, and the apocalyptic racket of a bumblebee bedevilled him awake. His legs and muzzle whiskers twitched with dreams of stalking food and of lapping sky blue water. Once he dreamed of his father's white marble eye rolling across a black sky. It made him whimper in his sleep, then his eyes snapped open to broad daylight. He stood, shook himself, and lay down again.

A thread-waisted wasp caught his attention, and he watched it dig a hole. With the spellbound concentration of one who is idle, he minutely observed the wasp's lavish industriousness. Its wingless body, covered with fuzzy hairs, was a warning red; its head and legs were black. Either oblivious of or indifferent to his immobile presence, it worked away less than a foot from the rim of Brand X's shady crater.

The wasp dug with its front legs, making dirt crumbs fly. Brand X recognized its digging as a miniature version of something he himself did. When the hole was the desired depth, it went down in it and began removing minuscule pebbles, carrying them out one by one in its jaws, dropping them, then going back down for another. When the bottom of the hole was cleared of pebble rubble, it dragged over a green caterpillar which it had killed with its potent sting.

Brand X saw that the wasp's intention was to push the dead caterpillar vertically down the hole, but its inert bulk was too ungainly to maneuver. The wasp changed its approach and straddled it, inching the caterpillar awkwardly forward beneath its body; but it still couldn't make the caterpillar slant downward into the hole. Leaving the caterpillar at the edge, the wasp went down the hole and, standing upright, reached up and seized the end of the caterpillar in its jaws and yanked it. The length of the caterpillar slid down the hole and disappeared. Brand X blinked. What he had taken for the wasp giving up had in fact been another change of tactic, a burst of inspiration.

It took the wasp a suspenseful amount of time to emerge from the close-fitting hole, because first it had to get out from under the smothering weight of the caterpillar it had pulled down upon itself. So caught up had Brand X become that, when the wasp finally did climb out, his tail softly thumped the ground in greeting. The wasp sat back to clean its face with alternating front feet. It then picked up in its jaws one of the pebbles it had removed and used it to tamp dirt into the hole. The hole closed, its task finished, the thread-waisted wasp walked away, leaving behind the egg which, unseen by Brand X, it had laid in the hole.

How many hot, shady hours Brand X had whiled away in his hideout in just such engrossing, random ways! Watching the comings and goings and doings of small beings passing by his nose; watching them admiringly, inquisitively, with a readiness to learn, intrigued by the ingenuity of others' solutions to crucial problems. The stress and hardship of crossing the sun-dazed lands would make him recall with amazement having once had the leisure to indulge in such trivial pleasures as watching a thread-waisted wasp dig and stock a hole and groom itself.

When shadows had stretched nearly full-length, Brand X stood up, shook himself, and left his hole under the double-trunked paloverde for the last time, tacitly bequeathing it to whatever being laid claim to it. Since it was a time of last times, he decided that before leaving he would make a complete round of his scent posts. Born of the universal urge to record one's passing presence, he wanted to leave behind fresh scent on each of his markers. He set off at a brisk trot. He had miles to cover.

He had not visited some of his scent posts in quite a while. He could tell by how faded the scent of his urine had become on them. On several of them—the mesquite log, the leaning paloverde, the mineral-striped rock, the rusty exhaust pipe, the hackberry bush, the fallen saguaro—he smelled the scents of passersby overlaid on his own, the scent of their urine as explicit as surveyors' garish ribbons tied to bushes. Each scent brought forth in his mind's eye an image of the coyote who had left it. He sniffed, sometimes cursorily, sometimes carefully, the information contained in the graffiti of their scents, and from it he learned who had stopped there and how long ago.

He began the climb up the mountain to his rocky outcropping. The fish fossil was always the last scent post he stopped at on his evening round. On the slope, little stalks of dried yellow fluff grass poked up between the small, gravelly stones lightly imbedded in the buff ground. Scattered atop them were larger rocks, broken-off hunks and chunks from the heights of the mountain.

When he reached the rocky promontory, he sat down beside the fossil rock and took up, for the last time, his languid vigil of the desert spread out before him. He did not sit there with a sense of being master of all he surveyed; it was not a question of mastery but of scenery. This was, quite simply, the spot from which his world looked best of all to him.

He gazed out across the narrow valley to the mountains opposite, their buttes, domes, and jagged ridges as familiar to his eye as the contours of his sun-hideout hole were to his body. He took it all in: the wash with its tributaries; the old paloverde nursemaiding the saguaro that had grown up through its protective branches; the scurrying forays of the little beings; the shack and the trailer of the old two-leggeds.

From this height, the grain of the desert, shown in the parallel, pinkish gray grooves of the washes, was as evident as the lie of a creature's fur. The cohesive fittingness of everything revealed itself to his eye: the way tributary, little washes joined the main wash; the way each saguaro, cholla, barrel cactus, ocotillo, creosote bush, brittlebush, smoke tree, mesquite, and paloverde stood solitary and discrete so that its roots had exclusive claim to each and every raindrop falling on or stored in the ground surrounding it.

Brand X tried to shake off the sense of betrayal that was working its way into him like a cholla thorn in a paw. By leaving for Skywater, he was abandoning his home ground. He knew that water would again cascade over the cliff with the window rock, refilling the catch basin, but he would not stay to wait for it. And even now his clawed paws could always find the right spots to dig wells which would fill with seepage, but, with his spirit set on Skywater, seepage now seemed paltry to him. He thought about the spendthrift water in the water-trails when the quick, hard, summer rains came and the profligate springtimes when the tawny land was miraculously meadowed with wildflowers, splashed with the enormous, impossible blossoms of the cacti and the red-orange slashes on the ocotillos' whips, and the yellow-bloomed paloverdes loud with bacchanalian bees. The highest treason of all though was that, in going to the ancient homeland of the stone fish, he must leave it, his place-sharer, behind.

He touched his nose to the fish's skeletal head and laid his muzzle across the delicate scratches of bone pressed into the stone. Beneath the light imprint of the Skywater being, deep within the stone, pulsed the muffled heartbeat of the ancient sea. His own heart spoke.

Little cousin, it said, I am going to your home. There are no trails for me to follow. Spirits leave no tracks. I will have to make my own trail. If I do not reach Skywater, if my path ends in the sun-dazed lands, I hope that a piece of mountain will lie down hard on my bones and take them into itself, the way this rock took your bones into itself. I hope that whoever finds my stone bones will know them, as I have known yours, as having belonged to a being whose thirst was not only in his mouth but in his spirit as well.

Brand X raised his muzzle to the sky, empty of the sun, empty still of the moon, empty even of the earliest stars, and from a heart aching with farewells but set on Skywater, he gave voice to himself. His farewell song arched across the blank desert sky like a jet's long vapor trail, high, continuous, and soon faded away.

7

One ought not to have to care
So much as you and I
Care when the birds come round the house
To seem to say good-bye . . .

ROBERT FROST, "The Hill Wife"

Albert Ryder, dozing on the bolted-down car seat on the breezeway, jerked awake. Although the howls that had awakened him seemed ubiquitous, he knew to look up the mountain to the rocky outcropping. And, yes, there he was: Brand X, with his howling head thrown so far back that his ears gave no silhouette to the sky. Albert reached into his shirt pocket for a cinnamon ball.

Hallie Durham Ryder hobbled out from her trailer and stood on the front stoop with a honey strainer in one hand and the mesquite walking stick in the other. Her face had the enraptured attentiveness of someone hearing a sentimental favorite.

"What the hell's gotten into him?" Albert said. "He hasn't made a ruckus like that since the day I dumped the shit in the tank."

Hallie shook the strainer at him to shush.

"Well he hasn't," Albert said defiantly.

From the far side of the shack, out by the mesquite tree

near the dry tank, an answering chorus of howls and yips broke out.

"The coyotes! They're back!" Hallie said in a voice that said how much she had missed them.

Albert grabbed his sailor hat off the nail. Although the sun was down, force of habit made him reach for the hat before leaving the breezeway. Even half asleep in the dead of night, he put on his hat before stumbling outside to relieve himself. Albert walked far enough out from the shack to see around it to the tank.

"Holy shit!" he said. "Come here quick."

Hallie got herself down the step and limped as fast as she could, babystepping, shoulders rocking, head bobbing, out to where Albert stood. Seeing what he saw, she said reverently, "In all my born days!"

By ones and twos and by families, the coyotes had gathered at their former water-place. Bred of an urge arising from long-standing habit, a habit which, like Albert's snatching his hat off the nail although the sun was down, served no purpose since the tank was dry, Dinty Moore had been drawn back at sundown to the place where he had once known security from thirst, drawn back in the eleventh-hour, if-only hope that the water tank might have been refilled and he would be spared the appalling journey to which he had committed himself.

The other coyotes, noticing the purposefulness of Dinty Moore's trot and the direction in which he was headed, trailed him there, thinking he knew something they didn't, thinking perhaps their longtime water-place had been restored. They had lowered optimistic muzzles into the tank only to find dried, decomposed droppings and some mesquite seed pods blown from the nearby tree.

When Brand X began his farewell howl, the coyotes were loosely ringed around the water tank, and his mournful voice spoke to their own despair at finding the water-place dry. Some of them gave voice to long, drawn-out, melodious howls; others only yipped, like a stammer that never becomes a full-fledged word; still others yipped as a preface to a series of howls; but, one way or another, each of the coyotes answered the lamentation coming from the silhouette of Brand X up on the rocky outcropping.

"What's gotten into them!" Albert said. "Coyotes don't bunch up like that."

"Shoot, don't ask me," Hallie said, "but it sure looks like they're asking us plain as day to fill the tank for them again. And I would, too! I'd pour every one of those goldurn water bottles into that tank if I thought it'd do any good!"

"Well it wouldn't," Albert said. "We couldn't afford to keep it up steady, so there's no sense in raising up their hopes by just doing it the once."

"I know that, Albert. But, Lord, I've a mind to!"

"All *I* know is I'm mighty glad to see them."

"That's right. If this isn't a Sunday, I don't know what is." Hallie turned around and hobbled off lopsidedly toward her trailer.

"What are you going to do, go curl your hair?" he grinned.

"This calls for a celebration!" she called over her shoulder and let the screen door bang behind her.

She came out with two chunky glasses which had sun-baked over the years to a milky turquoise. She had splurged them brimful with a mead she brewed from her bees' honey. It was the only kind of alcohol she touched and then only on a day deemed by her a Sunday, a day lifted high above the ordinary. She handed Albert a glass then raised hers toward the howling, yipping coyotes congregated around the rusty water trough and still higher in a salute to Brand X up on the mountain.

"Here's to you," she said. "We sure do wish you well, and

we're just sorry as can be that we can't fill up that tank for you."

"Yup," said Albert, holding out his glass at arm's length toward the coyotes, "it sure is good to have all my old drinking buddies back again."

Standing out there on the desert they had bought but did not consider themselves owners of, standing out there under a show-off sky which seemed loath to call it a day and get on with the business of night, Albert and Hallie Durham Ryder stood elbow to elbow and, over the chorus of coyote voices, reminisced about the generations of coyotes they had named and watered, those absent and those gathered before them. They recalled a charming rascal, a bully, an outlandish cut-up, good mothers and a bad one. They recollected lineages, injuries, come-uppances, merciful deaths and anguished ones. They noted who was missing and who was still around. They were surprised to see that the undersized, emaciated yearling named Boyardee had managed to last this long. He had survived the distemper he had had as a pup, but it had left him too slow-witted to fend adequately for himself.

"Poor little thing," she said. "He's not long for this world. Just as well, pitiful as he is."

Hallie was glad to see that the coyote named Kraft was still going strong. Since he had lost a leg in a trap about the time she had taken on her mesquite walking stick, she liked to claim three-legged kinship with him.

Albert laughed and swatted the air remembering the time Dinty Moore had tangled with a badger, and his mate Valvoline, wanting no part of such foolishness, had trotted away, throwing him a disgusted look over her shoulder.

"I'll never forget the look on her face if I live to be a hundred!" Hallie said.

"And you will."

"You bet I will! I'm too mean to die," Hallie chortled, the goodness of her heart stamped all over her old face.

Albert drew a blank on some of their names and had to ask Hallie. It wasn't just that it had been several months since they had stopped giving water to the critters. He never had been as good as Hallie at remembering them.

"I forget what you named that pretty little sister of Salem's. Something funny-sounding."

"Chieko," Hallie said. "From that candy-bar wrapper I found lying like a doormat in front of a packrat's nest. Lord only knows how a candy bar made in Japan wound up clear out here!"

They hadn't talked so much in months. As Albert had known would happen, without the critters to talk to each other through, they had kept their thoughts and worries to themselves. Since Albert was still spry enough to be out and about rockhounding, he had brought Hallie news of the coyotes he spotted, but it annoyed her to be dependent on his scanty reports. He didn't notice the things she would have noticed, and their names often escaped him. She could have kept track of them with the opera glasses she used for birdwatching, but she said it wasn't the same as seeing them with her own bare eyes and, besides, it made her feel like she was spying on them. And so to Hallie, critter-lonely, the gathering of coyotes around the water trough was as bountiful an event as a far-flung family's coming together in its entirety around a holiday table.

It was above all to Brand X, their unabashed favorite, that their attention and reminiscences were drawn again and again. As she looked up at his classic silhouette on the rocky outcropping, the gathering of coyotes at the dry water tank seemed under his aegis. They recalled the first time they had ever seen him and wounds they had watched heal and smart things they had seen him do. The honey homebrew loosened up Hallie's tongue, and she found herself telling Albert a thought she had harbored.

"I guess it's because of his javelina upbringing and his way

of keeping to himself, but I think of Brand X as being a critter at large," she said. "It's like he's got something over and
above about him that makes him not just one certain kind of
critter but like all these desert critters of ours all rolled into
one."

"Hogwash!" he said. "He's coyote through and through."

"I know that, Albert," Hallie said. "But you tell me why
Nabisco follows him around like a puppy dog. You tell me
that."

"It wasn't but a couple of times we saw that mustang trotting along after him. And, anyhow, saddle horses and dogs
have been known to make friends. It ain't so unheard of as
you're making it out to be."

"Well, all I have to say is a mustang isn't a saddle horse and
a coyote isn't a dog. I think Nabisco took a liking to Brand X
because he doesn't think of him as being just another coyote.
He thinks he's something special."

"Well, he is," Albert said, then muttered into his glass,
"but not in the fool way you're talking about."

Albert polished off his homebrew and banged his chest
with his fist, inducing a belch. It was something he hadn't
done in her presence for so long—she had always looked
primly offended by it—that it immediately reminded her of
how splendidly funny their son Pete had thought it was when
he was a baby: Daddy socking himself to make a bullfrog's
rumble come out. The memory of little Pete's mirth made
her feel lenient enough to offer Albert seconds.

"Help yourself," she said. "It's up there on the shelf with
the snake-bite kit."

"Good place for it. This stuff sure puts my sipping-
whiskey to shame."

His refill of honey homebrew, the sunset's radiant after-
math, his wife's face looking like Christmas morning, the
reunion of coyotes around the water tank, and Brand X in

howling-coyote silhouette up on the rocky outcropping combined to set off Albert, inspiring him, too, to give voice to himself. At first with the bashful awkwardness of a seldom singer then with devil-may-care abandon, Albert Ryder stood in the desert that had once been the floor of an ocean and tenored the sea chanteys he carried in his head like precious souvenirs brought out only on momentous occasions. Outward-bound and homeward-bound chanteys levitated through the strata of memory laid down by eighty-one years of living and burst forth into the desert air.

His sea-fevered singing made Hallie's heart feel girlish and adventurous; but when he threw his arm around her stooped shoulders and pulled her in against his side she shooed him off, flustered with shyness.

The coyotes broke off their howling. All at once Albert found himself left singing loudly alone. Feeling foolish, he stopped immediately, tossing the sea chanteys back into the attic trunk of memory and slamming down the lid on them. He scowled at the coyotes whose sudden silence had doused his high spirits.

"*Now* what's got into them," he grumbled.

"Don't ask me, but it looks like they all of a sudden caught wind of something. See how they've got their heads all raised up, sniffing and looking around every which way?"

"That's it!" he said. "Brand X. See there? He's gone." He pointed to the promontory where Brand X had stood. He had vanished.

Hallie chuckled. "So the choirmaster slipped off and left the choir singing their fool heads off without him!"

"Old Dinty Moore looks like he's about to bust a gasket over it."

"Well, you know how he is when it comes to Brand X. Always trying to tag along after him. Won't take no for an answer. Just look at him go scooting off!"

"And the others chasing after him like they want to get in on whatever it is, too." Albert cupped his hand around his mouth and shouted, "Hey! Where's the fire?"

"Well," Hallie sighed, "it sure was nice to have them back again."

"What's for supper?"

"Macaroni and cheese."

He nodded as if he had expected her to say that, then wiped homebrew off his mouth with the back of his hand.

"Seafood!" he said. "That's what I feel like having. I sure would like some seafood. Singing those chanteys always did give me a hankering for it. I've got half a notion to go to that cafe in town and get me some."

"Have you lost your mind, Albert Ryder? Drive seventy-eight miles round-trip for a piece of frozen fish?"

"Not just fish. *Seafood.* Food from the sea. Oh forget it. It was just an idea. Macaroni suits me fine."

Contrite over her quick rejection, Hallie slapped his arm and said decisively, "Shrimp. That's what I'm going to have. Fried shrimp! What about you?"

"The same," he grinned. "Maybe two batches."

"And I'm having a chocolate sundae for dessert."

"Ice cream! I'd forgot about there being such a thing."

"I think about it every so often—peppermint in particular—but, I swear to goodness, living out here makes anything that cold seem just as farfetched as seafood. Now aren't we a pair! Ice cream and seafood!"

As the last, dusky remnants of the sunset finally conceded to the encroachment of night, a seagoing pilgrimage set forth from the cactused desert of the Kofa Mountains. For Albert and Hallie Ryder, the journey's end was a plate of fried shrimp, with a wedge of lemon and two little pleated paper cups, one of tartar sauce, one of cocktail sauce, at the Hi Jolly Cafe in Quartzsite, Arizona. For Brand X, the journey's end was the glittering blue immensity of Skywater itself.

8

Born of the sun they travelled a short while to-
wards the sun,
And left the vivid air signed with their honour.

STEPHEN SPENDER, "I Think Continually
of Those Who Were Truly Great"

Downhill, his instincts told him. Follow the path that water
takes. Spirits going to Skywater do not leave trails. But water
does. His destination was the same as that of all water:
Skywater. He would seek it as water itself did, by going always downhill. Never mind that the sun guzzled it long before it reached there. The dry paths of once-water showed
where it sought to go.

Trusting his instincts, Brand X trotted lightly down the
gently sloping little wash. When it joined a wider one, he,
too, joined it, making himself like flowing water that knows
the way to Skywater. His trot was steady but not wastefully
brisk. He had set himself a good pace for going somewhere
far-flung. He was panting softly. He never once looked back
at the coyotes strung out behind him in the dry wash. He was
on his own. He was the leader of none.

Dinty Moore headed up the single-file line of six coyotes to
safeguard the gap between Brand X and them. Since it was
the ancestral song which he had flung into the sky from the

water tank that had alerted the others to Brand X's departure, Dinty Moore sensed it had fallen to him to protect Brand X's isolation.

Kodak was trailing Brand X only because he wanted to be there to lord it over him when he turned back from this arrogant journey; but the fluidly decisive manner of Brand X's gait dismayed him. It was as if Brand X were following a fresh scent trail that led straight to Skywater, a trail Kodak's nose could not detect. Three-legged Kraft didn't care where Brand X was headed. He was simply game for adventure, and, since it had been a long time since he had caught a jackrabbit, he was hoping that perhaps jackrabbits elsewhere wouldn't be as quick as those on home ground. For Salem and her sister Chieko, each of whom harbored the hope of becoming Brand X's place-sharer, trailing Brand X was a whither-thou-goest journey. Brain-damaged little Boyardee didn't know why he was trotting down a wash, but it was enough for him that others did.

The procession of coyotes came on the mustang stallion Nabisco and his band of three mares grazing on stray weeds in the wash. Their heads jerked up at the sight of so many coyotes passing by. The mares neighed skittishly. Although Nabisco did not understand the songs of coyotes, thirst is the common language of desert beings, and the purposeful way Brand X was trotting along, with so many others trailing him, told Nabisco that his destination must be a fine water-place.

Nabisco urgently needed to find a new water-place for his mares and himself. Their necks could barely reach down to the water in the bottom of the stone catch basin, and if their front hooves slipped over the slick rim of the water hole, they would fall in, break their legs, and die a long, bad death. When Brand X came trotting by, Nabisco did not see just a coyote. He saw the answer to his water problem.

The mustang respected Brand X as a finder of water. He had once seen Brand X dig up water in the dry bed of a wash just as if it were a bone he had remembered burying there. After Brand X had lapped the water and gone away, Nabisco had come out from under the mesquite tree where he had been standing and had lowered his nose into the hole and drunk, too. He had also found out that, by lifting his nose and waiting, a little more water would seep into the hole. Then he had become impatient with how slowly the hole filled and how small the amount of water was, and he had tried to make more water seep faster into the hole. A swipe of his clumsy hoof had destroyed the coyote well. Since that time, if he happened to find Brand X trotting in a wash, he followed him.

After the last of the string of coyotes had gone by, Nabisco whinnied to his lead mare to round up the other two, and the band of mustangs, with Nabisco bringing up the rear, set off down the wash. Boyardee spun around at the sound of their hooves noisily crunching the pebbly bed. Terrified of the massive, looming shapes, he pulled his tail between his legs and dashed ahead to trot beside Chieko.

As time went by, each coyote came to a certain place in the dry water-trail he had never gone beyond before, the invisible, personal boundary of his home ground. Wherever it fell, a prickle of awareness passed along his spine as he crossed it and became an outsider. No matter that the mountains still looked the same, that the gritty wash felt the same underfoot, and that the cacti, bushes and trees—taken one by one—looked like the ones just back across the border. On the far side of a boundary, nothing at all was the same. It was not home ground. It lacked meaning.

A saguaro looked just the same, but it was not a meaningful saguaro. It was not a saguaro to get one's bearings by. It stirred no memories of a squirrel eaten beside it, of a chase that had ended at it, of how a particular star sat at the tip of that curved arm at a certain time. No one knew who lived in the woodpecker holes drilled in it, and the holes in the banks of the wash and the paw prints pocking the sandy wash also belonged to unknown beings. Nothing here belonged to them, not the paw prints, not the holes, not the scent posts: nothing. All of the knowledge, intimacy, memory, understanding, and experience they could bring to bear on their home surroundings was irrelevant here. Nothing obtained. All was new, unknown, unfamiliar, and strange: *meaningless.*

By the time the last of the coyotes had crossed his boundary, the night air was pungent with the musky odor of fear coming from their scent glands. Smelling the others' fear buttressed Kodak's faltering resolve to continue, but the imagined pleasure of scoffing at Brand X when he turned back was fast dwindling into a silent, whiny plea that he just do so—and quickly. The only way Kraft could stave off the dire warnings of danger his heart was banging was to think about how good a jackrabbit would taste. Little Boyardee's fear scent was triggered simply because he smelled that the others were afraid of something.

Brand X readily identified the individual scents, each as unique as a fingerprint, making up the chorus of fear-odor, and thus he knew, without once turning his head, who of his own kind was trailing him: the companion-seeker, the challenger, the two sisters, the leg-lacking one, and the puppy-minded one.

Brand X was finding he rather liked the prickly, estranged, spinal sensation of being beyond his territory. It made official the status that had always had internal truth for him. But, oddly enough, now that his status was shared with the coyotes strung out behind him, he found himself experiencing an inchoate sense of camaraderie with them. He was an outsider among outsiders.

Dinty Moore was the first to spot the moon as it cleared the saddlepeak of a mountain. He yipped exultantly. The moon's appearance gave a tremendous lift to the tagalong coyotes' flagging spirits. With the moon overhead, the unknown land now had some vestige of home-meaning.

Brand X had not thought about whether his father's white marble eye would watch over him during his journey, but, seeing it, heavy-lidded tonight, with only a curve of white showing beneath the lid, he was glad of its company.

Far into the night, having dropped from twenty-six hundred to fifteen hundred feet, the wash Brand X had been following joined a very wide, steep-banked one. He halted at their juncture. The many tire-tread imprints in the pinkish gravel of the wide one indicated that this stretch of it served as a road. His pricked ears caught a buzzing hum. The tire tracks and the incessant hum made him uneasy. He climbed out of the wash to take a look around.

A signpost planted in the ground at the top of the bank a little farther downstream caught his attention. The sign was at a place where the bank tapered down low and the tire tracks left the wash there and continued on a dirt road paralleling the wash. He understood the bright, viscera red of the sign's words as he did the red of a velvet ant's body to be a warning. Stiff-legged with caution, he approached the sign, sniffed the wooden post where it went into the ground, then lifted his leg and passed water on it.

ENTERING ACTIVE MINE AREA
Use Extreme Caution!
Do Not Leave or Turn Off Road
BLASTING!!!

He turned toward the buzzing hum and saw, a quarter-mile away, three floodlights on tall wooden poles garishly illuminating a chainlink-fenced compound. The hum he was hearing came from the generator which ran the lights. Two sides of the fence climbed the skirt of the mountain that fanned out from the bare rock higher up the slope. The timber-framed entrance to a mine was centered in the exposed rock of the mountain. The excavated innards of the mountain were heaped on both sides of it. Dump trucks, backhoes, bulldozers, and skiploaders hunkered haphazardly within the fence—some up by the mine, some down below on the flat ground near the padlocked gate. A trailer which served as the mine's field office ran alongside the lower fence.

Because of having watched Hallie come and go from hers, Brand X recognized the trailer as being a shelter for two-leggeds. He also recognized the three little suns stuck up in the sky on tall poles as having to do with two-leggeds. He had often seen Albert and Hallie push back the would-be night with lanterns, flashlights, and campfires.

He knew that the tire tracks came from the once-removed way in which two-leggeds could move about quickly, making tracks not with their own feet, as other beings do, but with the vehicles they rode within. Only a snake or a creature dragging an injured leg left an uninterrupted, continuous track like a vehicle's; but a snake or an injured leg left a narrow furrow, not a broad band like a tire's track.

It was also the lack of any interval in the generator's steady hum that told him this was one of those once-removed sounds two-leggeds make not with their own mouths but with something of their own making. After a cactus wren, mustang, coyote, or any other being speaks, there follows a pause to listen for an answer, an attentive silence.

The fundamental meaning of the tire tracks, the sign, the hum, the machinery, the trailer, the floodlights, and the fence was plain to Brand X. This was a place of two-leggeds. It didn't matter that he neither heard, saw, nor smelled a single one. This place belonged to them as surely as his enlarged badger hole had belonged to him even when he wasn't lying in it.

Brand X heard the panting of the coyotes down in the wash. Heard the mustangs yanking up stray weeds and chewing them with their noisy teeth. Heard Salem growl at Kodak. Heard Kraft whine with longing for a jackrabbit. Heard Boyardee whimpering like a pup. He wanted them to be silent as stones.

Keeping his eyes warily trained on the fenced compound, Brand X backed up to the bank's edge and glared a summons down at Dinty Moore, acknowledging his trailing presence for the first time.

Called upon, singled out by the one whose companionship he wished above all else to prove worthy of, Dinty Moore scrambled to his feet, his mouth pulled back in a submissive smile, his low-held tail wagging desperately. He clambered up the steep bank.

Brand X glanced at him, then swept a warning look over the coyotes down in the wash.

Scruffy Dinty Moore, vested with the authority of Brand X himself, jumped down into the wash and trotted importantly among the coyotes. Kodak bared his teeth at him but did not risk the noise of a growl. In the name of Brand X, Dinty Moore achieved silence.

Brand X jumped back down into the wash and, without a glance at Dinty Moore standing with softly wagging tail and expectant eyes, proceeded down the wash. The great width of this dry water-trail he took as a sure sign of its being the right path to Skywater, but loath to set his paws in the tire tracks or even in the space between their parallel, double trail, he hugged the bank, staying just outside the reach of the catclaws, hackberries, paloverdes, and mesquite trees sparsely lining it. The hum of the generator faded, and the only sounds were the soft *tchuk-tchuk-tchuk-tchuk* of paws

on gritty sand and the occasional hollow clatter of hoof striking stone.

Dinty Moore, with the righteousness of the anointed,
moved ahead of Kodak to resume his position as first in line
behind Brand X. Kodak shot Dinty Moore a fierce warning
look, then wheeled around and jostled Kraft, shouldering
him so roughly on his one-legged side that he had to make
wild compensation to avoid being toppled. Kraft snarled a
low, formal protest then dropped back behind Kodak.

Salem pressed forward as if to drive Kraft still farther
down the line, but, instead, suddenly pivoted and hurled
herself at the hindquarters of her sister Chieko, mounting
and gripping her from behind as she herself wanted to be
gripped by Brand X.

Chieko yipped with surprise and dragged herself out from
under Salem's awkward lunge. Pelvis bucking, vulva con-
vulsively puckering, Salem flung herself at her again. Chieko
ducked her hindquarters and, growling, swung around out
of Salem's reach.

At the sound of Chieko's growl, Dinty Moore spun
around. Having been delegated by Brand X to keep silence,
he feared reprisal from Brand X for his failure to do so. Since
it was Chieko whom he had heard growl, he rounded on her
as the culprit. She cringed, hung her head, and limply
wagged her tail. Then Dinty Moore noticed Salem hobbling
dazedly behind Brand X, and he glowered at her in astonishment.

Her neck was outstretched and her ears pinned back as if
she were hurling herself into a strong headwind, and, unable
to stop the spasmodic thrusting of her pelvis, her hindquarters looked buckled, broken. Her eyes had the hard,
burned-in glaze of something fired in a kiln.

Dinty Moore ran forward and brusquely cut in front of
Salem to reassume what he considered his rightful position

behind Brand X. Hackles bristling, eyes crackling, Salem snarled at him with possessive fury—possessive of the very sight of Brand X which he had blocked. Dinty Moore, fearing Brand X would whirl on him if he caused a commotion, gave way and relinquished to Salem his cherished place as first in line behind Brand X.

Although Salem's assault had taken Chieko by surprise, she was not surprised at her sister having done such a thing. It was in keeping with Salem's high-strung, headlong, obliviously reckless nature, a nature Chieko well knew. Roughhousing as pups, Chieko had soon learned that with Salem play quickly ceased to be playful, and long after Chieko had signalled concession, Salem still wouldn't call it quits; enough was never enough for her.

The same was true of the way Salem secured food for herself. Relentless pursuit was her only method. She didn't stalk and pounce or lie in wait beside a burrow. She ran down her prey, bowled it over, and bolted it alive, as if to devour its spirit as well as its body. Afterward, her muzzle would be smeared with a grin of blood and a leer of triumph.

Unlike her sister, far more of Chieko's food was won by patience and ingenuity than by hot pursuit. Chieko was expert at biding her time. Her concentration on her prey in the instant before she pounced was so absolute that she herself ceased to be. In this suspension of her being, she became the one she hunted: the pocket mouse, the cottontail, the lizard, the blacktailed jackrabbit, the ground squirrel. She felt their trembling terror, their frozen panic, their quivering vulnerability to her pounce, her teeth, her dog-clawed paws. It was as if her pounce were an attempt to regain her lost self that had become her prey. So at one with them was she that, at times, it was as if she need not hunt at all. The tenacious, thorn-sharp focus of her motionless presence willed her prey to come out of its burrow to her of its own accord: take me; I am you. As she ate the one whose life her teeth had ended, both her heart and her grateful belly sang its praises: thank you, little cousin, for ending your worthy path to become my food. After eating, Chieko's face bore an expression of poised composure tinged with poignance, the look of one made sympathetic to suffering by first-hand knowledge of it.

Chieko had been born into the litter of a mother who was not merely rough with her pups but abusively cruel, sharp of temper and of tooth. Chieko had tried to keep out of her mother's way and make herself small against the wall of the den; but her mother, as if goaded by Chieko's timid innocence, would single her out, seize her by the muzzle, lift her high off the ground, shake her until her entrails felt jumbled, then fling her against the rock wall of the den. Salem, taking her cue from their mother, had endlessly harried and bullied her, too, and egged on the others in the litter to gang up on her. Born a tolerant one, Chieko had taken it.

By eight months of age, all of the pups had been driven off—all but Chieko, who kept slinking back to the den. If her mother, her bastion of safety, could be so terrifying, how much more terrifying, Chieko had thought, must be the motherless world she was being driven into. Although grown now and living on her own, whenever Chieko saw or caught wind of her mother she could not stop herself from cringing and shutting her eyes as she had as a pup when facing her mother's unavoidable, undeserved punishment.

As Chieko watched Salem trotting dazedly behind Brand X, she saw that her sister was bent on having him as her place-sharer, riveted on him with the same single-minded intensity with which she ran down her prey and gobbled it up, body and soul. Chieko, too, longed to have Brand X as her place-sharer, but flagrant pursuit was not her way. Her self-effacing shyness dictated that she wait for him, patiently but keenly, the same way she lay beside a burrow, in the hope that the power of her yearning would draw him to her.

But the fact that she was pitted against the ruthless passion of her sister filled Chieko with bleary despair, and, as she trotted down the dry water-trail, she mourned in advance her anticipated loss of Brand X, place-sharer of none but a stone fish.

9

Never morning wore
To evening but some heart did break.

ALFRED TENNYSON, *In Memoriam*

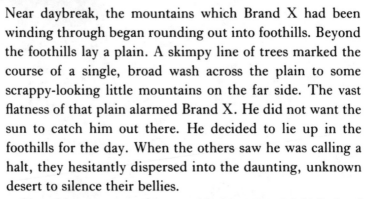

Near daybreak, the mountains which Brand X had been winding through began rounding out into foothills. Beyond the foothills lay a plain. A skimpy line of trees marked the course of a single, broad wash across the plain to some scrappy-looking little mountains on the far side. The vast flatness of that plain alarmed Brand X. He did not want the sun to catch him out there. He decided to lie up in the foothills for the day. When the others saw he was calling a halt, they hesitantly dispersed into the daunting, unknown desert to silence their bellies.

Since his tongue was longer with thirst than his belly loud with hunger, Brand X set out in search of water. If he happened across a jackrabbit or a pocket mouse, fine, but water was what he wanted above all. He backtracked to a place up the wash where, in passing, he had noticed a wide array of fresh tracks, scat, and scents. Guessing they would lead to a water-place, he began to follow the trail.

Nose to ground, he trotted briskly along the scent path,

raising his head every now and again to get his bearings in the landscape at large. The trail went in and out of small arroyos with trivial banks almost flush to the ground and climbed a saddlepeaked mountain. A cascade of rocks and boulders attested to the force of the water which, during rains, funneled down it from the top. The scent trail wove in and out of this tumble of mountain rubble and ended at a rocky catch basin under the overhang of a great slab of rock near the top of the narrow cascade. There was water in it. He lowered his muzzle to drink.

Out of nowhere, a snarling coyote rushed toward him, blind-siding him from upwind. He was considerably smaller than Brand X, but the element of surprise and the righteousness of his wrath at discovering an interloper at his waterplace were on his side.

Brand X, obeying the instinctive protocol for outsiders, flopped onto his side, opened his hind legs wide, and pulled back his head to expose his throat.

The snarling coyote lunged for Brand X's throat. At the last instant his muzzle veered upward. He haughtily circled Brand X several times to prolong the procedure, then leaned in to give him a perfunctory sniff and stood back, granting him permission to stand.

Brand X leaped to his feet. Fury scorched the edges of his politeness. He had come far, and he had great water-longing. He turned his back on the coyote and began lapping water.

Awestruck by the stature and bearing of the standing Brand X, faced with Brand X's obvious natural superiority, the coyote saw his circumstantial advantage disappear, and his eyes became flustered and unctuous. He trotted down the mountain uncertainly. Every few steps, he turned his head to look back at Brand X drinking from his water-place and tried to comprehend how it had come about that it was he who felt like an outsider and Brand X who seemed at home.

He suddenly saw six more outsider coyotes come out of the wash down below and begin threading their way straight toward him up the cascade of rocks. He reared back on his haunches with alarm then raced back to Brand X, who was standing stock-still, with raised head and dripping muzzle, watching the approaching procession of coyotes.

The coyote threw himself at Brand X's feet, rolled onto his back and exposed his throat to beg forgiveness and protection. Brand X eyed him with contempt. The coyote flinched when Brand X lowered his head and sniffed him cursorily. He stepped back to signal permission to stand. When the coyote continued to lie there, Brand X impatiently swiped him with a paw. The coyote fumbled to his feet.

But the arriving coyotes had already seen him. Seen him groveling before Brand X, throwing himself on Brand X's mercy. Seen him, at his own water-place, going through the self-abasing formalities required of an outsider. They sneered at him, then grinned at Brand X with admiring wonder.

The coyote ran off, zigzagging down the mountain as if under gunfire. When he reached the bottom, he turned back to deliver a face-saving growl then thought better of it and jumped down into the big wash to lie low until their scent became as faint as a wing's trail in the sky.

Salem pranced coyly up beside Brand X and tried to nibble his white-furred cheeks. He jerked back his head and bumped her roughly aside. She blinked hard, then flung herself down and twisted around to lick herself with nervous urgency. Throwing her a furrowed glance, Brand X wheeled on Dinty Moore for not having stopped her and the others from following him. He jabbed his nose at them.

Kodak, glaring his nonrepentence, lowered his muzzle and drank from the catch basin. Little Boyardee, failing to grasp the reprimand, smiled at Brand X and began to noisily lap water alongside Kodak. Kraft, by way of apology, turned and hop-loped on his three legs a short distance away. Dinty Moore flopped down disconsolately by an ocotillo to wait his turn to drink.

Chieko crawled under a brittlebush, lowered her head to her paws, and castigated herself for having followed her sister to Brand X. Her sister, like water rushing by in a full water-trail, could not be stopped, but was she herself nothing more than a stick carried on her fast waters? She had *known* her sister had been wrong to trail him here. She had *known* he would be angry at having been followed. She had *known* he wanted solitude. Why then, she asked herself, had she, knowing better, followed him, too? The ache within her was answer enough. Cringing in disgrace under a brittlebush, Chieko craved invisibility—but longed to be noticed by him.

By the time Brand X came across the jackrabbit, he was almost full enough not to bother with it. It had turned out that mice were numerous in this place, and his pounces had been accurate. He had eaten not amply but sufficiently; amplitude—except of sunlight, heat, sky and space—was something unknown to Brand X. Kodak had pursued the same jackrabbit a short while before, and, having escaped his teeth by only a hair's breadth dodge, it was so exhausted that Brand X took it with ease.

Since the mountaintops to the east were already outlined with light, he decided to take the jackrabbit with him rather than eat it on the spot. He carried it in his jaws by the middle of its limp back. Even so, he had to hold his head high to keep from stumbling over its dangling hind legs and outsize ears.

Brand X would have preferred to spend the hot hours under a paloverde tree up on a mountain slope, but since the dry water-trail was the way to Skywater, he felt compelled to stay near it. He chose a creosote bush at the top of the bank and, sniffing carefully at each of the holes which had been dug under the matrix of its exposed roots, found they belonged to kangaroo rats. Since they, too, were night-beings, he would be lying on top of them down in their burrows. Should their antic curiosity get the better of them, they would provide some amusement—food, too, perhaps—during his lie-up hours. He curled up under the creosote bush with the jackrabbit in easy reach and closed his eyes. He paid no attention to the mustangs browsing down in the wash nor to the other coyotes settling in for the day under nearby brittlebushes and creosote bushes.

Where Brand X lay, all was still in shadow, but up on the mountains spills of newborn light mellowed the rocks. A raven, spotting the hoarded jackrabbit, circled high above on sun-glossed wings. Brand X dragged it in closer to himself under the creosote bush, snapped at the pestering flies it attracted, and dozed.

While the sun climbed the slick, blue sky, he slept—sometimes lightly, sometimes deeply—in the lacy, breeze-flickered shade of the creosote bush. He went on a sleep-journey and roamed around his home ground. He visited his rocky outcropping, the water-place of the two-leggeds, his hole under the double-trunked paloverde, and the stone fish. When the journey ended, he enjoyed a floating interval of half-asleep in-betweeness in which the desert where he lay sounded so identical to home—a cactus wren's sprightly song; the rustlings of lizards dashing about under bushes; a mourning dove's call; the singsong of gnats; the hollow thonks of a Gila woodpecker hammering a saguaro; the cry of a red-tailed hawk—that he was momentarily lulled, still half-asleep as he was, into thinking that he was indeed home.

When he then came fully awake and found himself lying not, after all, under his double-trunked paloverde but under a gangly-rooted creosote bush and saw, rearing up before him, mountains of unfamiliar shape and color, he was jolted to realize he had been duped by a dream. Only the sky—taut blue, without a wrinkle of cloud—looked the same as at home.

While the others slept, Salem worked slavishly on enlarging and deepening a hole she had found. Every so often, she would stop digging, turn around and around in it, trying it out, then, still dissatisfied with it, dig at it some more. It seemed that she knew exactly how she wanted it to be but could not get it right. Having always been catch-as-catch-can about her daytime shelters, her sudden perfectionism was odd.

At last she gave up on the badger hole and began excavating a new one under a catclaw tree. Little stones and sandy soil flew between her hind legs. She dug and dug at it, apparently unable to make this one meet her suddenly finicky standards either.

Chieko lay under a dying paloverde which was densely festooned with parasitic mistletoe and watched her sister. She could not figure out why she was going to so much trouble to make a shelter that would be used only this once. Such elaborate efforts were justified in making a den for a litter, but there were no pups within her sister. She did not even have a place-sharer. But why did she keep licking herself so urgently? Why was she digging holes in such a frenzied, possessed way? Chieko decided it must be homesickness.

As the sun intruded by slow degrees into the coyotes' makeshift shelters and poked their eyes or pierced their fur, they were obliged to move from bush to bush, tree to tree. After several hours of such shifting about, it happened that all of them, each in the dappled shade of his own hideout, were gathered in a loose arc.

Within the sun-filigreed shade of his creosote bush, Brand X raised his head and looked around as if impatient to locate someone. He yipped abruptly at Chieko and nosed the jackrabbit away from himself.

She suspended her soft panting and swung her head to look at him, incredulous it could be her he had called to. Their eyes met briefly. She saw his ears pulled forward, awaiting her response. She tried to avoid looking at the dead jackrabbit.

Brand X nosed it farther away from himself.

Chieko trotted out from the shade under the paloverde. Her eyes slitted against the glare of open space and of envious eyes watching her from patches of shade. Kodak growled as she passed by, and Salem stopped digging long enough to give her a malicious glance. Kraft moaned softly. Boyardee licked his chops and wagged his tail. Dinty Moore looked despondently back and forth from the jackrabbit to Chieko.

A jumble of thoughts and hopes ricocheted in joyful confusion within Chieko, but she presented herself matter-of-factly at Brand X's creosote bush. Her mouth filled with drool at the closeness of the jackrabbit, but she did not look at it.

Her quiet decorum irritated Brand X. Why didn't she just snatch it and run or else roll over in slavering gratitude? But no, there she stood, as if politely seeking clarification of his intention. He considered revoking his offer just so as not to have it misconstrued by her—and those watching others. But misconstrued as what? He was not giving her food—he told himself—but ridding himself of an annoyance. The flies would go with the jackrabbit.

Chieko stuck her head under the outer branches of his creosote bush and grasped the limp jackrabbit. As she backed out with it, she raised her eyes and found his watching her. What she saw in his eyes warned her not to express gratitude with hers. He lowered his head onto his forelegs and closed his eyes, as if to demonstrate that, with the removal of the fly-magnetic jackrabbit, he could, at long last, get some sleep.

She was almost back to her paloverde when she heard Brand X behind her. She turned with the jackrabbit dangling from her mouth, her jaw already slackening to drop it in case he had changed his mind and wanted it back. Kodak, seeing her grip loosen, dashed out to snatch it from her. Brand X whirled around and, his back hunching and jaws gaping, sent Kodak slinking back into the shade, then he trotted past Chieko as if she weren't there, passed water against a white bursage, and returned to his creosote bush.

She lugged the jackrabbit into the shade under her mistletoe-choked paloverde and, using her paws to brace it, tore solemnly into it.

Dinty Moore let out a long moan. Chieko lifted her head to look at him. He grinned at her and wagged his tail eagerly. Remembering that it was Dinty Moore who had alerted her to Brand X's departure, she pulled out a wad of innards and nosed them toward him.

Dinty Moore darted out of his hideout. Kodak snarled at him but stayed under his brittlebush. Dinty Moore trotted to Chieko's paloverde to claim the gift pile of innards. He gobbled them so fast his teeth barely touched them. Licking his chops, he fixed a longing gaze on the remainder of the jackrabbit firmly fastened under Chieko's forepaw, then he noticed Brand X's head turn toward him and his brows pull together in a glower, and, with exaggerated dejection, Dinty Moore returned to his creosote bush.

Suddenly, on the opposite bank of the wash, a local mustang sounded a shrill challenge to Nabisco, who was dozing under a mesquite with his three mares. He jerked awake, wild-eyed. The coyotes jumped to their feet and stood with craning necks and pricked ears, waiting to see what would happen next and whether it would be anything of benefit to their bellies.

Star Kist, the lead mare, tossed her head nervously and

nudged and nipped the other two mares farther down the wash. She knew what was coming: a battle for ownership of her and the other two.

Nabisco whinnied sharply and lunged up the steep bank. Pawing the stony ground, the two stallions appraised each other. Nabisco was a buckskin with dark mane and tail; the other stallion, a bluish-gray with a hairless, white zigzag scar along one flank. When the stallion had come on Nabisco, dozing with droopy neck down in the wash, Nabisco had looked so old and lackluster that the stallion had assumed the takeover of the mares would be easy, that the old one would do no more than put up a brief, halfhearted show of resistance, then flee. Seeing him now, with head high, eyes fierce and nostrils flanged, the local stallion's confidence slipped.

Nabisco charged forward. The stallion met his charge, and, ears flattened, the two mustangs reared and lashed out with their hooves. Teeth bared, they dove for each other's legs and necks, whatever their teeth could grab and sink into. They ducked and whirled and veered, looking for openings, seeking advantages. A roiling, gritty fog of dust enveloped them. When they rammed into cholla cacti, they were oblivious to the pain from the fist-sized clumps of hooked barbs which broke off and imbedded in their hides.

Overwhelmed by the unexpected strength of his adversary, the stallion was about to turn tail and gallop away when Nabisco, in dodging a donkey-kick, got a foreleg down a hole, stumbled, and fell to his knees. With Nabisco down, the stallion saw a happy ending in store after all. The stallion reared once more, just for good measure, and brought his flailing hooves down on Nabisco as he lurched to his feet. Nabisco managed to duck free of the forelegs straddling his neck, but his leg, twisted by the hole, buckled under him. Limping heavily, he backed away, his sides heaving and lathered, his neck lowered: defeated.

The stallion leaped triumphantly into the wash to claim the three mares. They clustered together, milling, skittish of the meaning of the battle's outcome; they were now his. He whinnied exhortations to Star Kist to get the others moving. He bit her flank hard to hurry her up. She screamed, and her brown eyes momentarily rolled white. It spooked the other mares, and they fled down the wash, Star Kist trailing them. The victorious stallion chased after his battle trophies.

Nabisco nickered forlornly to his vanished mares. He plunged down into the wash as if to follow them, but his injured leg made him pull up short. He limped aimlessly back and forth across the wash, halfheartedly lipping brittle weeds and jerking up his head to listen for the longed-for sound of returning hooves.

By now, the sun had slid so far down the sky that its light struck only the flanks of the mountains, leaving the narrow valley of the wash in shadow. The coyotes, agitated by the stallions' battle, emerged from their shelters and headed for the catch basin where they had drunk that morning.

Chieko had saved a jackrabbit haunch for Brand X. It was still fur-covered except where it had been torn free of the body; on that part, the red gloss of the exposed meat had become dull and crusted from the day's heat. She studied it as if to determine whether or not her good intention merited the effort of lugging it all the way up the mountain to the waterplace. With a deep sigh, knowing there was no way except in her own jaws to safeguard it, she picked it up, and, its long foot bumping her chest, started off with it. As she threaded her way up the cascade of rocks, every so often she had to stop and set down the haunch in order to be able to pant.

Brand X, who had observed her indecision over the haunch, came alongside of her and reached out his muzzle toward it. She dropped it as if she had stolen it. Brand X seized the haunch and gave her an acknowledging, sideways glance.

After drinking from the catch basin, he trotted off across the mountain slope to a rocky outcropping reminiscent to him of his lookout post at home. He wanted to study the flat desert plain they would be crossing that night and to map it on his mind's eye. The thought of having to be out there in the flats disturbed him. So, too, did the confounding reticence of the solemn-eyed guardian of the jackrabbit haunch. He shook off with difficulty the urge mounting in his chest and congealing in his throat to give voice to the unexpected vulnerability they had brought forth in him.

10

*Thou hast heard, O my soul, the sound of the
trumpet, the alarm of war.*

JEREMIAH

The signs posted at measured intervals on the boundary
fence out along Highway 95 warned:

KEEP OUT
U.S. GOVERNMENT PROPERTY
Trespassers Will Be PROSECUTED
U.S. Army Test and Evaluation Command
Yuma Proving Ground
FIRING RANGE

But, following the same broad wash he had joined back in the
Kofa Mountains, Brand X came in far to the east of Highway
95 onto the remote back portion of the Yuma Proving
Ground. The wash bisected the desolate, vast plain of the
military installation's entire fifty-six mile width.

He now clung to the wash not only because it was water's
trail to Skywater but also because only there was he out of
sight of the enormous, ominous, effortlessly domineering,
night-silhouetted hulks that made his hackles bristle with
fear and suspicion. The tank chassis, car bodies, and armor

steel-plate walls he saw at regular intervals out on the flats were stationary targets for the experimental ordnance being tested at the Yuma Proving Ground. In places, piles of tumbled rock forced him to abandon the wash. Whenever this happened, his fear of the target objects made him cling so closely to the edge of the bank that twice, in spots deeply undercut by flash floods, the bank collapsed under him, plummeting him down into the wash.

Several miles into the proving ground, Brand X came to a culvert where a dirt access road crossed the wash. Neck outstretched, he warily approached the culvert pipe and sniffed gingerly at its galvanized steel circumference. Its entrance was partially blocked by a conical jumble of dead branches that resembled the disarrayed rubble of a packrat's nest. He stepped back to consider the meaning of this obstacle and found that, looking through the loose matrix of dead wood, he could see the water-trail resume on the other side of the pipe.

Nosing through the obstructing branches, he took two tentative, reluctant steps into the tunnel of the pipe. Its steel corrugations edged uncomfortably between the pads of his paws. He rounded his paws up from the intrusions, but that made his claws scrabble on the pipe's curvature. He backed out.

Dinty Moore slipped quietly alongside him to eye the culvert. Startled, Brand X jumped laterally; he had been concentrating so hard on the pipe that he hadn't noticed Dinty Moore's approach. Dinty Moore wagged his tail apologetically, but Brand X, angry at having been startled, gave him a threatening look and scrambled up the steep bank.

Brand X had just crossed the dirt access road when it came: an explosion; a devouring, cataclysmic, bone-rattling BOOM, and, with it, as thunder's twin is lightning, a sight-annihilating flash of blue and white light.

The obliterating light and noise—the seeming totality of *all* light and *all* noise—hit Brand X. Blind and deaf, he fell to the ground in a frantic sprawl. His feet scrabbled frenziedly in the gritty ground to anchor themselves to something, anything, to keep himself from endlessly falling into the silence and blackness, the non-ness, into which he had suddenly been hurled.

It was the claustrophobic, unmitigated black of his blindness that terrified him the most. This blindness was of another kind altogether than the light-innocent blindness of a newborn pup. This was the terror of knowing his eyes were open—blinking and blinking to make certain that, yes, they *were* open—but that open or shut made no difference. This was not the black of fur, of night, of obsidian, of wet ironwood. This was not the color black. This was the black of void, of *not*.

After a period of time without any bearings to measure it by, Brand X began to dimly discern shapes and found himself lying in front of the culvert pipe on the far side from where he had left the others. In his panic-stricken blindness, he had stumbled off the bank and fallen down into the wash. He shook his head and rubbed his forepaws over his ears, trying to hasten the restoration of his hearing and night vision. At last, he heard, in the muffled way of the partially deaf, the forlorn cry of one who has abandoned hope of being answered but nonetheless continues to call out. He recognized the voice as Chieko's.

He bellied through the culvert, his previous fear of it forgotten. He reached the matrix of branches caught crosswise across the upstream end of the pipe and started to push through them. When the branches didn't yield, he realized it was because they were being held against the opening by the pressure of something on them. He shoved his nose into the space between two branches and sniffed: Salem.

When the flashfire and the explosion had burst upon her, Salem had lurched forward, blinded and deafened, and run up against the tangled deadwood clogging the entrance to the culvert pipe. She was frantically working her way into the branches as if to make a haven of them when her nose had touched something soft. It was a glove, a work glove of gray cowhide and heavy, blue-herringboned cotton. After recoiling from its unexpectedness, she had been drawn back to it and pulled it free of the branch on which it was snagged.

In the darkness of her blindness and the silence of her deafness, the glove had become her link to the world which had, in a tremendous flash of light and tremendous burst of noise, ceased to exist. In her desperate need to attach herself to the lost world, the richly dense, nocturnal world of sights and sounds she had so suddenly been robbed of, the glove had become her anchor.

She latched onto it with fervent devotion, minutely exploring it with her nose and mouth, learning its smells, its textures, its tastes with the intimacy only the blind and deaf can know. It was the most elaborate thing her mouth had ever encountered. The undersides of the cowhide fingers were deeply grooved where finger joints had habitually bent. The suede fibers in the grooves of the finger joints were coarse, but the rest of the leather fingers were worn smooth and ingrained with glossy grime. The thumb and index finger were completely of cowhide; and it was to these, after trying the partially cotton fingers and the elastic band across the wrist, that she returned again and again. Her teeth discovered a small tear in the seam joining the cotton topside of the little finger to the cowhide underside, and she worried the frayed cotton edge until she had ripped the seam open.

As her hearing and vision gradually returned, Salem began to lick and groom the glove instead of gnawing and ripping it. By the time she felt the branches move against her as they were pushed outward by Brand X inside the culvert pipe, the glove had become something she was fiercely protective of. Holding it in her teeth by the thumb, she wriggled out of the network of branches, slunk dazedly off to one side, and lay with the glove fastened down with her paw.

Brand X braided through the tangled wood and emerged from the culvert pipe. Chieko, with an upsurge of joyful relief at the sight of him, forgot her shyness and ran to him with jubilant tail and softly rubbed her shoulder against his. Dinty Moore crowded around him, sniffing him all over. Kraft limped jerkily toward him on his three legs. Little Boyardee dashed to greet him as if Brand X were a father returning to the den with a rabbit hanging from his jaws. Kodak gave him a glance of hard appraisal, hoping to see signs that Brand X had suffered the same stark terror that he had.

During the remainder of the night there were other explosions, but they came from gun positions far to the west of Big Eye Wash. Even so, at each explosion, no matter how dulled by distance, Brand X froze, paw lifted, ears pricked, eyes fixed, waiting to see if he could still see, waiting to hear if he could still hear, before resuming his brisk, Skywater-bound trot down the dry water-trail.

I I

I love to lose myself in a mystery;
to pursue my reason to an O altitudo!

THOMAS BROWNE, *Religio Medici*

Out on the sun-seared flats of the Yuma Proving Ground, a new material for military uniforms was being tested, cannons and other towed weapons were being dragged about, weapons were being mounted on tanks, an experimental helicopter from the Castle Dome Heliport at Y.P.G. was being readied for testing, and medium, crew-served weapons were being fired into target objects. While one crew from Instrumentation went out to collect the data from the M-48 tank chassis that had been the target of the previous night's kinetic weapon's test firing, a second crew began setting up skygates for velocimeter testing out in the flats down range of gun site #25.

Throughout all of these activities, the coyotes slept fitfully, deep in the shade of a stand of salt cedars growing in the wash. The repercussion of the previous night's blinding, deafening explosion still resounded in them. Chieko whimpered with bad dreams, Kraft mouthed fretfully at his stump, Kodak was surlier than usual, Boyardee's eyes had a shell-shocked glaze, and Salem, still bewildered over whether the glove was food to be eaten or a pup to care for, alternately gnawed and groomed it. Remembering the explosion made Brand X's spirit shrivel within him, parched for Skywater, weary of wariness.

The skygates he had watched the two-leggeds erect out on the flats troubled him almost as much as the memory of the previous night's explosion. Ominously inert, implacably metallic, the two ladder-steel towers stood there, glinting in the sun, dangerously wrong-looking and too suddenly there.

The two-leggeds, arrogant of the heat that had sent all other creatures scurrying for shade, had come out in broad, blazing daylight to construct these sudden, enormous, inexplicable things which, as far as he could discern, had nothing to do with food, water, or shelter from the sun, and then had gone away and left them standing out there—defiant of the sun and impervious to time—where nothing else but white bursage and creosote bushes could withstand the sun's full brunt. All other creatures when they departed from a place left behind only their droppings, tracks, scent, and, finally, their bones; and, over time, all of these things disappeared.

Because he was already edgy, it was more than Brand X could stand when Salem left the salt cedar where she had been lying and, carrying the glove, trotted a short way out into the flats to lie in the shade under a tank chassis. He went to rout her out.

His lowered nose jerked back from a cigarette butt and a scatter of spent .30-.30 shells on the ground in front of the tank. He smelled birth and death. Smelled that a litter of pups had been born in the lair beneath the tank then killed in front of it. The history he smelled reeked of his brothers and sisters skewered out of the den into the glare of the world, then shot and gunnysacked.

Despite his horror of it, Brand X bellied halfway under the tank. Salem raised her head at his intrusion and moved her paw to cover the glove. Her tail hesitantly thumped the ground as she eyed him, unsure what to make of his appearance half in, half out of her dusky shelter.

He whined at her anxiously. She lowered her head to pull at the thumb of the glove with her teeth while holding it down with her paw. Although honored by his coming to evacuate her from a place he thought endangered, she was loath to leave the deep, solid shade of this low, strange shelter. Her tail beat a feeble apology.

Brand X backed out until only his head remained beneath the tank. She tugged at the cowhide thumb and watched him. With a growl he quickly bellied forward, snatched the glove from her, and scrambled backward into full sunlight. She yelped and scurried out after him.

With his hold over her established, he ignored her as he trotted back to the wash. The glove gripped in his jaws tasted wonderful. The stiff cowhide had been worked pulpy soft by her chewing and saliva. On his home ground, he had once come across a tooled leather belt and had spent one of the happiest days of his life chewing it right down to the big, bronco-stamped, oval buckle.

Whining pitifully, Salem trotted alongside of him and jostled him and swiped at his muzzle, begging for the glove. Brand X carried it back to the salt cedar where she had been lying before and, with great reluctance, dropped it. She pounced on it as if it might escape.

His bereft mouth watered. He wished the glove belonged to her sister, the one who had guarded the jackrabbit haunch for him. *She* would have gladly given him the glove. He wheeled on Salem with a warning growl to stay put, then trotted dejectedly back to his salt cedar.

A short while later, Range Control gave permission to the

artillery crewmen in the fire control tower at gun site #25 to open fire, and the cannon being tested was electrically fired from the gun site's bunker-like control room. For seconds after the enormous artillery projectile had passed through the two ovals suspended from the skygates, the BOOM hung in the air like an annunciating presence.

The coyotes sprang to their feet, then dropped into cowering crouches. In their attitudes of frozen motion—jaws clamped to silence panting; eyes fixed; ears forward—they looked like products of taxidermy in museum cases; but, while they stood dead-still, braced, their hearts raced headlong within them.

Only the battle-lame mustang Nabisco bolted out of the wash. He ran like an elongated shadow of himself out across the flats, his mane standing up like flames from his outstretched neck and the veins in his chest, neck, and shoulders standing out on his sweat-slick coat like subcutaneous vines, running until his lame leg reduced him to a lunging hobble.

An artillery crewman up in the fire control tower spotted him and shouted into his radio to Range Control, "Mustang! Down range of the first gate approximately five hundred meters and moving in a southwesterly direction."

"Roger, we see it. That one sure gave Tracking and Monitoring the slip! Their last report put the whole herd down toward the Muggins. Must of been down in the wash. Looks like it's got a bum leg. Well, it's clear of your test. Continue firing. We'll alert the V.H.E. Repeat: continue firing."

"Roger. Will proceed."

"Hang on! Hold your fire!"

"What is it?"

"Whole mess of 'em."

"What, mustangs? I don't see them."

"No. Coyotes. Down in the wash. You got 'em in your binocs yet?"

"Just a— Yeah! Yeah!"

"Well, hold your fire there till we get hold of Major Thurmond and find out what he wants to do about it. Alert your firing crew about the delay and stand by."

Major Thurmond, the pudgy, thirty-two-year-old head veterinarian at the Yuma Proving Ground's Veterinary and Health Environmental Office, leaned back in his swivel chair to consider the report he had just received from Range Control. In his pensiveness he forgot the nerve-shattering habit his chair had of precipitously rearing backward. Lurching forward, he grabbed the edge of his desk and waited for the queasy, falling sensation in his stomach to go away; then, hunched over, leery of leaning back, he reviewed the various elements of the situation: a gimpy, lone mustang out on the flats in the vicinity of velocimeter testing at gun site #25 and a pack of coyotes down in the wash nearby. Standard procedure dictated that whenever any wildlife—especially the federally protected species like the mustangs—was spotted in the line of fire, they were required to stop firing *if* the test was at a point where it was economically feasible to do so.

A *pack?* he thought. Not this variety of coyote, the Mearns' desert coyote. Rabies could account for it or, at any rate, go further than anything else he could think of to account for it, this assemblage of coyotes. Major Thurmond knew one thing for certain: there'd be hell to pay if a twenty-four-hour-a-day installation with five hundred personnel directly involved in testing got brought to a halt by some kind of epidemic among the wildlife. So, if diseased, they must be destroyed, for their own good and the safety of the personnel. A determining factor would be whether or not they showed fear of man. Rabid wildlife show absolutely no fear of man; it's a sure sign of their sickness.

Having reached a preliminary conclusion, Major Thurmond eased himself back warily in his swivel chair, careful not to exert that last bit of pressure that would send it rearing back. He notified Range Control to keep all personnel clear of the area where the coyotes were located and dispatched two of his special M.P.s to investigate the situation and report back to him by radio. Informally called "the major's dogcatchers," they were members of the Military Police detachment who had received rudimentary training in wildlife health and management.

The M.P.s drove downrange in an olive drab Dodge M-880 four-wheel-drive truck with a wire cage on the back. The access road they took roughly paralleled Big Eye Wash. Their instructions were to observe the coyotes to see if they appeared to be diseased and presented a clear and present health danger to crews working out there—and to take backup weapons.

"Great, just great," said Sgt. Olander. "Just what I always wanted to do, go check out a bunch of possibly rabid coyotes when it's 117 in the shade."

"Yeah, me too," said Sgt. Haley. "Hang on, we're getting close to where Range Control spotted the pack."

Sgt. Olander pulled to the side of the access road and turned off the engine. M-16 rifles in hand, they got out of the truck, unsnapped the holsters holding their .45 caliber automatic pistols, and, exchanging jittery grins, headed for the salt cedars growing in the wash.

Gun-cunning had come to Brand X the day he had watched the rancher shoot his brothers and sisters. Now, seeing the two-leggeds coming toward him with rifles, he burst from the shade of the salt cedar and fled, abandoning the wash to run out into the flats on the far side of the wash from the approaching two-leggeds.

"Hey! There goes one!" Olander shouted, raising his M-16 to point. "And another one. And *another* one. Goddamn, it *is* a pack!"

"Quick! Get a count. The major wants a count."

"I make it seven."

"Me, too. Seven."

"Hey! It's a three-legged one."

"Where?

"Third one behind that lead one. See it?"

"Yeah. Look at that son of a bitch go! I met a guy at a bar in Yuma couple weeks ago said he'd seen a *two*-legged one that could still run like a bat outta hell. I figured he must be bullshitting, but now I seen that one, maybe not."

"Jesus, what's that one got hanging out of its mouth?" Olander underarmed his M-16 to look through the field glasses hanging around his neck. "Hard to tell, but it looks like a glove."

"Think the hand's still in it?" Haley laughed.

"Well, let's radio the major. Fact they took off like that means we scared 'em good."

"So?"

"So no rabies. You heard the major. Said if they didn't scatter and run like hell when we approached then there was a good chance of it being rabies."

After running turntail out into the flats, Brand X slowed to a trot and then stopped and turned broadside to the two-leggeds standing by the truck. When fleeing from danger, he preferred to turn tail to it for as short a time as possible, because he had long ago discovered that the mindlessness of headlong, turntail running only served to enlarge his fear. After running a short distance from an immediate threat, he then always moved broadside to it, paralleling it to keep tabs on it from a safe distance.

When the M.P.s got into the truck, turned it around and drove back the way they had come, Brand X stayed abreast of it from afar. He looked furtive, almost cringing, as he moved along, head and tail pulled low, gaunt body slung like a slack hammock between the points of his shoulders and hipbones, turning his head often to gauge his safety from the truck. As he approached the barbed-wire-topped chainlink fence enclosing the power generation and amplification stations, he curved back toward the wash.

Major Thurmond studied the notes he had jotted from the report the M.P.s had radioed in. Trying to make sense of it all, he circled the 7 several times, then, tossing his pencil onto the desk, bellowed at a clerk for coffee. "*Hot* coffee for once, goddammit!"

When the coffee came he was lost in thought, and, taking a big swig, scalded his mouth. He spluttered it back into the cup, wiped the spatters off the notepad, and muttered ferociously, "Just what the fuck is going *on* around here?"

But then Major Thurmond remembered that at least he could rule out rabies. Across the top of the coffee-freckled page, he wrote "R/O rabies." Retracing the letters until they were thick and kindergartenish, he determined to do three things.

First, notify Range Control to keep an eye on the situation but to proceed with testing. Second, give Schroeder at Fish and Wildlife in Yuma a call to find out if anything unusual had turned up at the adjacent Kofa Wildlife Refuge: any disease going around; any unusual ecologic pressure that might explain coyotes forming what appeared to be a pack. Last, turn it over to Environmental. Now that *he* had ruled out any clear and present health danger to Y.P.G. personnel, let *them* try to figure out what the sudden appearance of a bunch of coyotes all cozied up together down in Big Eye Wash was all about. He tossed his pencil onto his desk and leaned back carefully in his chair.

By the time the sunset's last purple strands were blackening above the Chocolate Mountains on the Cibola Aircraft Armament Test Range on the other side of Highway 95, the seven coyotes had reunited three miles downstream of where they had fled the wash. On returning to the wash, the first thing each of them had done was dig for water near some salt cedars whose presence was a tip-off that groundwater lay near the surface; they were far too parched to care how saline the seepage was in the holes they had dug.

While the coyotes dispersed to hunt food, the mustang, having returned to the wash's salt cedars for refuge from the sun, discovered the wells the coyotes had dug and, hobbling from hole to hole, drank from each of them in turn.

When Brand X had caught just enough grasshoppers and mice to dull his hunger, he set off at an impatient pace, fervent to leave behind the desolate, sight-stealing, booming flats where gun-bearing two-leggeds braved the sun's fiercest stare. He craved mountains. To the south, squatting out in the flats like a geologic miscalculation, stood the Muggins Mountains, a mangy pittance of a range. But to Brand X, they were an inspiring, pinnacled goal.

12

Miss. Emily Wahl
314 N. Hillside Street
Manhattan, Kansas

Dear Emily,

I don't know if you're still alive or in a rest home or what,
but I'm writing you at your folks' house where I used to come
play because that's the only address I know for you.

I wish I could be there to see your face when you find out
that the bump in the envelope is those little bitty magnetic
Scottie dogs of yours! I bet you had forgotten all about them,
but I hadn't! Anyhow, here they are, just as good as new, the
black one and the white one both, still a-pulling and a-
pushing at each other. Nice thing about magnets is they don't
wear out like folks do!

I'm sending them because I want my conscience spick and
span when I go to meet my Maker. I still don't think I stole

them from you. You as good as promised them to me as payment that time I cleaned your closet and all that clutter under your bed for you. The fun I had with them was always kind of spoiled though, knowing I had denied taking them.

If you wanted a clean one yourself—a conscience I'm meaning, not a closet—you'd send those Scottie dogs right back, saying I was owed them all along. But just give them back to me in your heart and that will do fine. Anyhow, we don't have a mailbox.

Your old school friend,
Hallie Durham Ryder

13

I must not keep forgetting
I am still travelling
The land between here
And the sea.

GARY SNYDER, "Riding the hot electric train"

Dinty Moore, his tail wagging deferentially, moved up beside Brand X trotting down the wash. Brand X swung his head to see what Dinty Moore wanted: just to be alongside him, it seemed. But he noticed a tentative boldness in the gaze Dinty Moore returned. Brand X reprimanded him by opening up his trot, though only enough to put Dinty Moore's head at his flank. It puzzled him why Dinty Moore had now abandoned his vigilance over the gap which he had so conscientiously maintained throughout the now three nights of their journey, fending off at last even Salem from trotting too closely behind him.

Brand X turned his head to check that new look in Dinty Moore's eyes again. This time Dinty Moore's golden eyes flared with eagerness to please, and Brand X decided that the boldness in his eye had simply come from the courage it had taken for Dinty Moore to come up beside him.

Never before had Brand X trotted along with a fellow moon-caller stride-for-stride through the night in the reverberant, almost reverent silence that acknowledges a fledgling friendship. It made him ill at ease. He wanted to growl at Dinty Moore to get away from him and never again presume to come up alongside him like this; but, crowded though he felt and new though he was to the ways of companionship, a kind of instinctive civility held him back.

Having allowed Dinty Moore to remain at his flank, Brand X found himself forced to think about him, to *consider* him, as he never had before. He was astonished by how much knowledge of him he had unconsciously gathered over the years. He remembered when Dinty Moore had first come to his attention: the night he had listened to him calling out to the spirit of his place-sharer who had been shot that morning.

It was in autumn, when the creosote bushes were dotted with cottony white puffballs and the saguaros crowned with withered blossoms, that the hunters always came. Albert and Hallie's land was a private inholding within what had come to be the Kofa National Wildlife Refuge. Since they had neither the desire nor the money to fence it off, during the hunting season Albert and Hallie themselves became fences. Hallie went up and stood like a fence post atop a bird's-eye-view mountain and warned off trespassers with a homemade megaphone. Albert lit out across the desert in the pickup to chase off any stubborn ones who ignored her.

It was an anxious, exhausting time for Albert and Hallie, protecting the critters which, by living on their land, had unwittingly made themselves illegal targets. A state lottery determined the annual winners of permits to shoot a bighorn sheep from the refuge herd, but deer, quail, rabbits, gray foxes, bobcats, skunks, and coyotes were fair game for anyone with a firearm or a bow and arrow. And an unfenced inholding with nothing on it but a tumbledown shack and an old trailer was nothing hunters felt obliged to honor.

Of all the trespassers they had over the years none was more flagrant than the one who had crouched behind Hallie's trailer and shot Dinty Moore's mate, the one whom Hallie had named Valvoline, as she crested the bank of the wash to come drink from their water tank. Hallie, up on the mountain, had whirled around at the sound of the shot and the hunter's exultant whoop and looked down on the one place she had not watched because she had thought it surely safe: her own home.

"Valvoline! Valvoline!" she had cried out from the mountain.

The hunter, hearing her cry, had tipped back his head and visored his eyes. "Shit, ma'am," he yelled, "I didn't know he was a pet! I took it for a coyote."

"She's a *she,* you blindman! And she's not a pet! She was one of my *neighbors!* Now get out! Just get out, get out!"

Lying under the double-trunked paloverde on his rocky outcropping, Brand X had watched Hallie come avalanching down the mountain. And he had seen water come from her eyes, seen her face wet with water that fell from her eyes like rain from the sky. He had never known such a thing was possible—that eyes could make something as precious as water.

It was seeing her tears and watching her drive off the hunter—one of her own kind, a two-legged—by throwing big stones and loud words at him and then kneeling down by the coyote and stroking her fur—Valvoline lying in a heap, her legs jerking as they tried to keep up with her spirit racing to Skywater—that had convinced Brand X, once and for all, that this two-legged who had never seemed the same as others truly was different from all others. She was not an enemy.

That night, Dinty Moore's bereaved howling had gone on for so long that Brand X, himself a veteran of loss, had made a point of finding out who it was whose grief was so large it filled the whole sky.

Trotting down the wash, with Dinty Moore's head at his flank, Brand X remembered all of this, and he remembered, too, the recent dawn when Dinty Moore had waited for him by the dangerously depleted water hole in the slick redrock. He knew that Dinty Moore's lingering presence as he had pondered where to go from now on for water was partially responsible for his having reached the answer that had lain like groundwater deep within him: he would journey to Skywater.

Lost in thought, Brand X suddenly noticed the sound of panting close on his hindquarters. He wheeled around so quickly that Salem rammed into his chest. Seeing her burning eyes, he wondered for a moment if the panting he had heard had come from them and not from her mouth. He bared his teeth at her to drive her back, but he blamed himself for having allowed Dinty Moore to entice him out of his solitude.

He veered sharply away from Dinty Moore and, with lowered nose, tightly crisscrossed the wash, sniffing at rocks, then paused at one to pass a sibilant stream against it. He trotted away quickly, knowing that Dinty Moore and the others would be compelled to stop and pass water there, too, permitting him to re-establish the distance he wanted from all of them but the burning-eyed one in particular.

Dinty Moore watched disconsolately, knowing that Brand X had used the need to pass water as a pretense to drive him away. He passed an obligatory squirt against the rock and looked wistfully after Brand X, hoping for a head-turn of invitation that he knew wouldn't come.

Salem crowded in on Chieko as she squatted to pass water beside the rock and growled at her to give way, which she did. Salem dribbled a few drops onto the rock, then swung around to face Dinty Moore and, defiant of the taboo against it, stared him directly in the eye, searching for the reason Brand X had permitted him the position beside him which she coveted. Dinty Moore extricated his eyes from hers and trotted off as if from a close call.

When Kodak shouldered past Salem to reach the rock, it jarred her out of a fixed stare at nothing, and she broke into a lope to catch up with Brand X; but she stopped in her tracks when she remembered his bared teeth and the way his eyes had hardened against her. She gazed around dazedly, stunned with rejection, then climbed out of the wash as if she had been summoned and walked with stiff-legged formality to a rocky mound that looked like the false start of a mountain.

Climbing atop it, she dropped the glove, leaned back into her haunches, and raised her muzzle until her head was tilted so far back on her neck that her ears lay flat against it and the length of her throat was offered to the moon's white fang. She opened her jaws into a wide V, the scimitar curve of her eyeteeth perfect copies of the moon's luminous fang, and hurled her voice, her ululating, anguished voice, up into the black, star-speckled, light-freckled void guarded by the moon's sharp fang.

Brand X stopped to solemnly eye her up on the mound, then trotted away. The others threw uneasy glances at her and hastened after Brand X.

Only the mustang Nabisco, poised with raised head, flanged nostrils, and flicking ears, seemed to listen intently; but he was listening not to Salem's entreaty but for the voices of his mares. He had just caught wind of a herd at the base of the Muggins Mountains, and wishful thinking had made him forget they were way back in the Kofas and not out here on the flats. He decided to join the herd. The stallion leader would permit him to since, being lame, he presented no threat to him. He would have to lie low with the colts and the old stallions who had also lost their mares until his twisted leg was strong again. The thought of leaving the coyotes reminded Nabisco he was thirsty, and he hobbled off to catch up with their leader.

Brand X, hearing the clatter of hoofs on stone, turned and watched the stallion limp toward him. Nabisco nickered for his attention and pawed at the sandy wash with a foreleg until he had gouged out a crude hole. He lowered his head toward it to imitate drinking from it. Then he raised his head, tossed it impatiently, and again pawed the sand and lowered his head to the hole.

Brand X's eyes ignited with comprehension. He looked around for a likely spot and, turning his head every few steps to be sure the mustang was following him, went to an outside bend of the wash and began digging. The mustang, his head bobbing up and down with eagerness to drink, stood to the side of Brand X. At last, when his body was steeply slanted down into the hole, Brand X hit moist sand. He stopped digging and stood peering down into the well he had dug. Satisfied to see it slowly filling, he stepped aside. Nabisco came forward and lowered his nose into it and drank.

While he drank, Brand X reached out tentatively with his muzzle and touched the mustang's hind leg with his nose. The leg flinched at his touch, and the mustang's tail switched him in the face with its coarse, stinging hairs. Brand X jumped back. Nabisco swung his head around to regard him. A euphoric giddiness spread through Brand X at having dared to put his nose against this enormous, living creature's skin.

Dawn was not far off, and Brand X was determined not to spend another day holed up in the searing flats. He needed the respite of a mountain, the vantage point and spirit-food of a mountain. He mottled a rock with his scent to mark the

spot where he was leaving the water-trail. With a decisive-
ness that belied the backward glances of his instincts at leaving the water-trail that was the way to Skywater, he bounded
out of the wash and loped toward the mountains' burly silhouette.

Dinty Moore and Chieko exchanged startled glances and,
after quickly passing water on Brand X's marker, raced after
him. Boyardee whimpered with confusion and looked back
and forth from Kraft to Kodak for guidance. Salem, still atop
the rocky mound, snapped out of her trancelike stance as
Brand X passed by and, seizing the mangled shreds of the
glove, ran to catch up with him.

Brand X made for a notch in the dragon-spined ridge of
the mountain. When he gained the summit, he looked to the
south and, panting hard from incredulity as much as from
the climb, saw the Gila River and the vast grid of the Gila
River Project's irrigation canals and the solid, stunning, rec-
tangular green of cotton and alfalfa fields and grassy mead-
ows where cattle grazed. In the midst of the sparsest desert
he had ever encountered was the most abundant water and
the densest carpet of green he had ever beheld.

On his home ground, when there *was* water in the washes,
it was the sudden water of flash floods, a roiling, rusty porridge bearing uprooted trees, pack rats' labor-of-love nests,
small, drowned creatures, and anything else that got in its
prideful way; and, at home, when the ground sprouted
something green—weeds, fluff grass, Mormon tea—it was
sparsely spaced and soon sun-bleached to brittle, pale straw.
But the gently curving river down there at the base of the
mountains flowed calmly, its force siphoned off into the
linear network of tamed, orderly water lying languidly between concrete banks; and the fields and citrus groves looked
unnaturally, eternally green, beyond the reach of sun and of
season.

Brand X wondered if his eyes were mocking him. He had, on occasion, seen vast, shimmering water-places out in the distance, blue as the sky itself, and he had raced toward them, tongue lolling with anticipation, only to watch them evaporate before he could reach them. Instead of running toward them, he had tried stalking them, creeping up on them on his belly, the pads of his feet burned by the searing mosaic of flat, black volcanic stones on which the shimmering water-places so often appeared. He had tried feigning indifference to them, turning his back on them, then whirling around to catch them in the act of disappearing. But, no matter what he tried, they always dried up before he could drink from them. At last he had decided the false water-places were a joke, a cruel joke played on thirsty creatures by the sun, and he had disciplined himself to simply ignore them.

But the water down there did not quiver and, besides, the sun was still crouched down behind the land. Yet if he went down there to drink, believing the water would stay put, the sun might spring up and make it disappear. It was not worth the risk. Mirages had angered and frustrated him and made him feel foolish; but they had not piqued his curiosity and made a vapor of caution rise in him the way these orderly water-places did. He had learned the hard way to rein in his curiosity with caution, having found out that often the things which had piqued his curiosity, such as the skunk's and the scorpion's handstands, were the very things to be most wary of.

Dinty Moore came up into the ridge notch beside Brand X. Seeing the bounty of water and verdure below, he yipped in amazement, and his eyes filled with devout wonder.

Borne on updrafts of hot air from the valley floor, the fragrance of orange blossoms from the citrus groves filled their noses with an elusive smell. Brand X raised his muzzle and tested the air, jerking his head up and down to take short, rapid sniffs. Dinty Moore's jowls puffed in and out, and his nose, too, worked to trap it. The aroma didn't arouse hunger in them, but it smelled so tantalizingly good that they stretched their necks toward it as if it were food hanging from a branch just out of reach.

Since it reminded Brand X of the way his home ground smelled in the season when the paloverdes were yellow with blossoms and bees, he thought it must come from the trees growing in rows between the lines of the water-paths. This smell was thicker though. Its mesmerizing sweetness clung harder to his nose.

As they stood with slitted eyes and spellbound noses raised, the mournful wail of a distant, long-drawn howl came floating through the fragrance-laden air: the whistle of a Yuma-bound freight train home-stretching along the Southern Pacific tracks out in the flats along Highway 95. Brand X stood so still he felt as if he were swaying. Dinty Moore's hackles porcupined along his spine; he thought he was hearing the voice of an ancestral moon-caller.

The sun's blatant appearance broke their enchantment, sharply reminding them that, glutted though they were with sweet-smelling, watery, green, ancestrally howling wonders, their bellies were empty and mouths parched. Dinty Moore plunged downhill to drink from the irrigation canals, stopping midway to look back to see if Brand X was coming. Brand X checked his impulse to warn Dinty Moore to stay away from those somehow-wrong water-places.

Brand X caught and ate a cottontail rabbit and a white-footed mouse and then had the good fortune to surprise a big chuckwalla lizard. It was doing push-ups atop a sunlit rock to get its circulation moving, and he pounced on it before it could wedge itself into a crevice in the rocks. He was relieved that the blood and juices of his prey had provided sufficient liquid to quench his immediate thirst so that he did not need to go down the mountain to drink from the irrigation canals.

For that day's shelter from the merciless sun, Brand X selected the bare ground under the overhang of a rock slab halfway down the mountain's southern flank. The tracks, dried droppings, and shape-smells of other creatures informed him he was one of many to have done so. Lying beneath the eave of the rock, he looked down on the river and the irrigation canals and, beyond them, to the Gila Mountains. His gaze traced the wash he had followed so faithfully, and he saw that, although at this time of the year it had no water to contribute, its trail dead-ended at the river. It made Skywater seem closer to him knowing that, when he resumed his journey tonight, he would be following not the dry trail of water but water itself.

Yet, as he dozed intermittently under the stone eave, a vague sense of dread continued to nag at him. It looked so *crowded* down there—crowded with rows of water-places and close-together, good-smelling trees; crowded with herds of large, horned creatures with their noses buried in thick, bright green grass. The wide spacing of plants and creatures dictated by scarcity of water was all he had ever known, all that he understood.

And, too, the irrigation canals—even the river—had an aura of *ownership* about them that reminded him of Salem with the delicious glove. The glove was not hers; it did not belong to her as her fur and eyes and spirit did. She was only its finder. It was a windfall, like happening on a fresh carcass one's teeth had no exclusive claim to and which one therefore should not begrudge ravens, hawks, turkey vultures, and flies their fair share of, too.

Something drastic had happened to this desert land. It had been tampered with, irreparably damaged, like a mother nipping off her pup's ear-tip in her enraged impatience to make him behave. This was not desert. This was land no longer true to itself.

With uneasy eyes, he watched the coyotes drinking from the irrigation canals, trotting from one to another to prove to themselves it was actual water that could actually be lapped and reveling in having a bounty of water choices.

At last, his belly sloshing, Dinty Moore began working his way back up the mountain. Brand X, deep under the rock's shady overhang, watched him stop several times to peer around intently and test the air and knew that he was searching for him. When Dinty Moore finally spotted him, he made straight for him and, with a breezy assumption of welcome, flopped down in the shade of a young paloverde growing crookedly from a crumbled rock just to the side of Brand X's ledge. He was grinning with glee.

Brand X swung the golden suns of his eyes hard on Dinty Moore. To account for his gleeful grin, Dinty Moore pointed his nose down at the flowing river and the irrigation canals which had so thoroughly quenched his water-longing. And, seeing Dinty Moore as happy as a water-fat barrel cactus in bloom, Brand X felt miserly for having wanted him not to drink there at all.

14

Internal Revenue Service
Washington, D.C.

Dear Sir or Madam,

I am sending $40.00 in this envelope. I know you're not
supposed to send cash money in the mail, but I'm hoping
whoever opens this up is honest and that you'll do right by
me and turn it in.

I don't have any tax forms, but I wouldn't have the least
notion anyhow of what we owe. We haven't had two nickels
to rub together all these years, but we're plenty rich in sun-
rises and other such things that the government doesn't tax
yet. I came up with $40.00 by making it a dollar for every
year we've been out here in the Kofas and adding on one
more just for good measure.

I'm sorry I don't have two nice crisp twenty-dollar bills to
give you instead of all these wrinkled old ones and fives, but

this is what was in my honey jar. I am sending this money because I don't want to leave any debts owing behind me.

I thank you for your trouble.

Sincerely,
Hallie Durham Ryder

P.S. Don't worry yourself about a receipt. We don't have a mailbox.

 **15**

Unminded, unmoaned.

JOHN HEYWOOD, *Proverbs*

Shortly after sunset, when streamers of orange and red were flung across the sky, Brand X awoke, stretched, and came out from under the eave of rock where he had spent the day. He made a leisurely, last study of the terrain he would be crossing during that night's journey, mapping its features on his mind's eye: the irrigation canals bordering the green fields, the Gila River, and, to the south, the Gila Mountains.

His gaze furrowed at the four-lane highway he had not previously noticed out in the distance. From where he stood, the vehicles moving along it looked small and harmless as grasshoppers; but he wasn't deceived. He watched an elf owl fly out of a hole in a saguaro and take to the evening sky. He envied it the carefree, lofty ease and aboveness of wings that made crossing two-leggeds' broad, black trails no obstacle. He began zigzagging down the slope.

Dinty Moore stood up under the paloverde where he had been sleeping and shook himself. He yipped twice to alert the others scattered here and there on the mountainside to Brand X's departure and started after him.

Salem crawled out from the hollow beneath a slanted
boulder and, without even taking time to stretch or shake
herself, rushed after Brand X. Her paws dislodged small
stones lightly imbedded in the slope, and Dinty Moore
glanced uphill with annoyance to see who was sending them
rolling down on him.

He froze, paw in midair, at the sight of her oddly cumber-
some gait and her fur standing up in muddy spikes. Gooey,
gray shreds of cowhide from the glove hung from her lower
jaw like strands of viscous drool. Her mud-caked belly fur
dripped.

Giving her a wide berth, Dinty Moore climbed back up
the slope. He had to know how she had become muddy while
lying on a dry mountain. He sniffed a stone spattered with a
drip from her belly and, disbelieving his nose, licked it: *milk*.
He backtracked along the trail of her milk-drips to the shallow, cavelike hollow beneath the boulder where she had lain.
The lair was muddy with milk, the mud churned up and
grooved by her claws' frantic raking.

He turned to go and saw Chieko had been watching him
investigate her sister's lair. He gave her a warning glance to
prepare her for what she would find. He suddenly felt an
urgent need to reach Brand X before Salem caught up with
him, and he tore off down the slope.

Chieko slunk toward the lair as if she were under a curse to
go there. After a brief, horrified glance and recoiling sniff at
the milky mud, she sank back onto her haunches, overwhelmed. She was certain her sister had no place-sharer.
Neither Brand X, Kodak, Kraft, nor Dinty Moore had made
the slightest courtship overture to Salem. It was not the season for it. Yet, the milk was indisputable. It had to be that
the volatile combination of Salem's high-strung nature and
the force of her longing for Brand X had brought on this
phantom pregnancy, a counterfeit which so faithfully mim-
icked the genuine that milk had come into her teats.

Chieko bolted downhill to assess her sister's condition at close range. Salem whirled at her approach. Her lips drew back from her gaping jaws. Suddenly she blinked, pricked her ears, and cocked her head. Her furious gaze shifted away from Chieko and became unfocused in the manner of one listening intently.

Chieko cocked her head to listen, too; but all she heard was a black-tailed gnatcatcher singing a pretty little song. Shaken, she watched Salem plunge down the mountain as if in answer to a summons.

Dinty Moore overtook Brand X as he neared the bottom of the mountain. Brand X swung an irritated glance toward him, and Dinty Moore found himself confused as to what was so drastically crucial about a milk-drizzling, mud-caked coyote after all.

Salem, jaunty with pride at thinking herself summoned, trotted up and faced Brand X. The involuted abandon in her eyes, the drool-like strands of mangled cowhide dangling from her jaw, her tawny fur spiked with muck, and her engorged teats spilling onto the ground made her jauntiness chillingly grotesque. She wagged her tail.

Brand X gave her a cold look of inquiry. Her gaze faltered. He stared for a few moments at her milk spattering onto small stones and pocking the ground beneath her, then he trotted off toward the river, throwing her a single, backward glance of repulsion. Gaunt-eyed, she hunched into a cringe.

Dinty Moore averted his eyes from her humiliation and edged away. He saw Chieko, poised with lifted paw on the slope, scrutinize her sister as, tail drawn between her legs, lethargic with despair, Salem dragged herself off after Brand X.

Cottonwood trees flourished four and five deep along the banks of the river, and, as he passed among them, Brand X registered with wonder the extravagance of their big, green leaves. Desert trees—mesquite, paloverde, ironwood, smoke trees—had to economize and make do with little vestigial ones.

Standing on humped, water-smoothed stones settled in mud, he lowered his head to drink from the river. He had never drunk from a river before; it seemed to him an honor to do so. He drank for a long time. Every so often, he raised his head to look upstream and downstream in astonishment at the river's unassuming, continuous presence. Because he did not feel hurried to drink from it before the sun or others guzzled it up, he noticed its taste. It tasted very good to him.

The others, who had drunk there early that morning, already took the river for granted, and Kodak, seeing there was enough water for all, didn't try to hoard the river for himself. Lined up along its edge, they lapped matter-of-factly, but their sidelong glances of appraisal at Brand X's initiation to river water recaptured their own previous elation.

When he had finished drinking, Brand X went and sat under a cottonwood tree to study the river from the standpoint of its being a barrier that must be crossed. Now a controlled waterway, the Gila River's sluggish waters were a far cry from the wild river it once had been, rushing toward confluence with the once-mighty Colorado. Nonetheless, to Brand X, who had never swum nor seen another being swim, its watery width was formidable. The fish fossil on his outcropping had taught him nothing about how it had once moved through water.

He trotted along the lush, wooded, weed-green bank until he came to a place where a low, metal catwalk crossed the river. Sitting back, he eyed it intently for a long time, trying to determine if its usefulness in getting him across the river outweighed its dangerous unfamiliarity. The others, who had by now drunk their fill and hunted or foraged along the bank, began to pace impatiently in small, nervous circles.

A pickup truck turned onto a dirt service road which paralleled one of the main canals and headed toward them, its headlights shoving aside the night. The catwalk and his ignorance of swimming forgotten, Brand X plunged into the river, and the others splashed in after him.

Having never swum, Brand X found himself swimming. He tipped his muzzle so far out of the water that he saw the moon above him. His legs ran through the water as though he were running on land, but the water's resistance against his legs and the lack of solid ground beneath his paws gave him the frightening sensation that his running was futile.

The pickup that had catalyzed their crossing swept by, its Mexican driver muttering curses in Spanish about the busted sluice gate his boss had sent him out after dark to fix. The headlights' swath did not take in the river.

When his paws touched bottom, Brand X was jolted by the hardness of ground after the suspension of water, and his legs felt rubbery as he waded out. He shook himself and turned to look at the river whose width he had swum. He saw a random pattern of upthrust, wedge-shaped coyote heads jutting above the river's moon-striated surface, and he shuddered at the memory of his father's disembodied head.

Kodak, Dinty Moore, Salem, and Chieko were nearly across, but Kraft and Boyardee were having trouble getting out of the midstream current, mild though it was. The running motion of the stump of Kraft's missing leg was of some use in water, but, even so, having only a single full-length foreleg made it hard for him to stay afloat. Boyardee, weak with starvation, had become so exhausted that he kept trying to rest his chin on the surface of the water. When his muzzle sank and he inhaled water, his damaged mind could not fathom why, and his eyes became wild with terrified confusion.

One by one, all of the others except Kraft and Boyardee

waded out and shook themselves. Their wet fur clung to them, making them look pathetically bedraggled and diminished. Jubilant over their successful crossing, Dinty Moore, Chieko and Kodak frisked high-spiritedly on the bank. Although Salem did not join them, she appeared more normal with her fur washed clean of the spiky muck. Their fur dried fast in the hot, dry air, restoring the illusion of prosperity to their skeletal frames.

Kraft's and Boyardee's paws touched bottom at nearly the same moment. They exchanged a look of startled joy at having underfoot the solid ground which they had despaired of ever knowing again. They dragged themselves forward into the shallows and collapsed, too exhausted to climb onto the bank. Their panting wheezed.

Brand X stood apart, thinking of the other river still to be crossed, the broad, black highway flowing with sudden death. He was jarred to find himself vicariously enjoying the others' cavorting and relieved at seeing Kraft and Boyardee safely ashore downstream; but, like a father monitoring a hawk's shadow wraithing over his pups as they tussle, innocent of the world's dangers, in the springtime warmth outside the den, his knowledge of what lay ahead for them tightly noosed the moment. He waited until Kraft and Boyardee had summoned the strength to rejoin them before he set out toward the highway that lay in his chosen path like a dreaded, inevitable snake stretched to its full length.

When he reached it, Brand X crouched behind a creosote bush just back from the shoulder of the highway. The others lined up on either side of him behind other creosotes. They cringed back into their haunches when branches whooshed by the air turbulence from a double-trailer truck whipped them in the face.

Twice, Brand X was gathered to dash across the highway when a new batch of headlights appeared, coming on faster than he had thought possible. He reared back as the trucks whumped past, shuddering at the certainty that, had he gone, he would not have made it to the other side.

Traffic at night on this stretch of Interstate 8, thirty miles east of Yuma, was fairly steady. Refrigerated trailer trucks used I-8 to make night-runs across the desert floor between Tucson and San Diego. Night-runs also reduced the risk of overheated radiators for the heavily-laden campers, cars lugging motor homes, and vehicles of uncertain reliability. Their brakes pungent from having just come down the steep grade of Telegraph Pass, westbound trucks roared by in the lane nearest the crouched coyotes.

At last, a coinciding break in the traffic on both sides came. Brand X hurtled into it, running so fast the pads of his paws barely registered the sun's stored heat still radiating from the black pavement. While he had waited, he had singled out an ocotillo directly opposite himself on the far side of the highway and had decided it was to that ocotillo he would run with his life. Now his elongated body stretched toward it as if with yearning for its crooked, woody wands tipped with last spring's flaming flowers now dried and faded. As he ran toward it, the ocotillo comprised his entire world, a world that grew in height and detail as he bore down on it.

When he reached the ocotillo, he spun around as if to take on some dire creature that had relentlessly pursued him to prevent him from reaching it. Moonshadows of the ocotillo's towering wands fell across him, striping his fur as if marking him as its own.

With the exception of Boyardee, the others had leaped forward the instant they had seen Brand X burst from behind the creosote bush, and they too, as soon as they gained safety, whirled to face the wide, black highway as if it had been a cougar snapping at their heels.

Boyardee had gotten off to a late start. Still overwhelmed with exhaustion from crossing the river, he had lain down on his side behind a creosote bush and closed his eyes. Once, when a car nicked the shoulder and pelted him with gravel, he was too dulled with starvation and fatigue to even flinch. The other coyotes had understood, as Boyardee had not, that Brand X was waiting for an opportunity to cross the highway. They had stood with hair-trigger attentiveness, fully primed to take off running as soon as Brand X did.

By the time Boyardee had wearily half raised his head, the others were already lunging after Brand X. Energized by the fear of being left behind, he scrambled to his feet and started across at a wobbly trot just as Brand X reached the median strip and the headlights of an oncoming vehicle crested a slight rise.

When the other coyotes had reached safety and spun around as if to face a cougar, it was little Boyardee they saw on the highway. They leaned into him with their eyes, willing him to hurry as the headlights grew brighter. Boyardee crossed the median strip and started across the two east-bound lanes. His emaciated body, bushy tail, and long-muzzled profile, picked out by the headlights' wedge, took on such clarity of definition it was as if he were the intended focal point of a spotlight. His baffled eyes seemed to occupy all of his delicate face, making his face scream with eyes. He turned his head and squinted into the glaring wedge bearing down on him, then, overwhelmed with light, huddled on the pavement.

The wedge of light came from a Ford pickup with a camper mounted on it. Below the Oklahoma license plate, the rear bumper was plastered with overlapping bumper stickers from Yosemite, the Grand Canyon, Fisherman's Wharf, Knott's Berry Farm, and Hussong's Cantina. Wildlife decals framed the camper's aluminum-scrolled screen

door: a mallard in flight; an upright black bear; a buck with a
full rack; a running roadrunner; an arching rainbow trout; a
lolling-tongued, cartoonish coyote; a coiled rattlesnake.
Diagonally across the camper's top left corner was hand-
painted "Hank & Noreen" and across the right rear corner
"The Tiltin' Hilton."

Noreen's hand shot out to grab her husband's arm as the
headlights nailed a huddled animal with lightstruck eyes
turned fully toward them.

"Hank! Watch out!"

There was a thump.

"Oh God! You hit it! I felt it! You hit it!" She covered her
mouth and swivelled her torso to see it, forgetting that the
camper blocked her rear view.

"Pipe down!" he said, sluffing off her hand. "It was nothing, just some varmint." But he glanced surreptitiously in his
sideview mirror to see the small heap, then squared himself
self-righteously on the seat, shifting his buttocks and thrusting his shoulders.

"Varmint! How do *you* know!" she said. "Those eyes! I
never *saw* such eyes! Just like one of those pictures on those
greeting cards."

"Pictures? *What* pictures! What the hell're you talking
about?"

"Oh, *you* know. That box of greeting cards I bought at
Fisherman's Wharf with those great big sad-eyed little kids
looking right straight out at you. They were selling framed
pictures of them, too, and I said to you, I remember clear as
day, I said, 'Hank, I swear the eyes in that picture are following me all over the store.' *Now* you remember?"

"You've got it all screwed up. It was the *Jesus* plate that
had the funny eyes that followed you around," he said, glad
for the argument because it helped to settle the burp of conscience in his belly over that huddled animal he'd run over.

"Well, anyhow, you didn't have to hit it. All you had to do was swerve a little bit."

"If I'd of *swerved*, we would of *flipped*, Noreen! You think you'd feel sorry for that varmint if we'd of flipped out here in the middle of fuckin' nowhere in the middle of the fuckin' night all because some varmint didn't have *brains* enough to stay off the fuckin' *inter*state? Give me a Tums. You got a Tums?"

"Yeah, back there in my makeup case." She jerked a thumb over her shoulder at the camper.

"Well, shit, why don't you keep them up here in your *purse* instead of all that other crap you got in there that makes it so heavy I gotta drag it around for you every time we stop?"

The mention of the Jesus plate reminded Noreen that today was Sunday, although it didn't seem like it since they hadn't gone to church the way she had promised her pastor back home she intended to while they were travelling. Thinking about church, she forgot about the huddled animal with the lightstruck eyes and, after a little while, couldn't remember what it was that had started their silly argument.

She picked up the Tiltin' Hilton's mascot which was perched between them on the seat. Called a jackalope, it was a stuffed jackrabbit with antlers attached to its head so realistically it looked as if they had sprouted there. The sunglasses on it were Noreen's inspiration. At the R-V parks where they stopped for the night, they got a kick out of showing it around to folks, some of whom sort of *thought* their leg was being pulled but weren't entirely, one hundred percent sure.

Noreen lightly poked Hank's overhanging belly with a prong of the jackalope's antler and, pretending to be speaking for it, said in a low, jolly voice, "Say there, Hank! What say we stop at the next Stuckey's and get us some coffee and let Noreen make wee-wee and get you those Tums?"

Hank, grinning despite himself, pushed aside the jack-alope and said, "Last one to spot Stuckey's has to lug in your goddamn purse when we get there."

Boyardee was lying on his side with his head thrown back and his eyes open as if staring with longing at those who had reached safety. They knew there was no reason for them to try to prod him into rising or to sniff him for a glimmer of life. They knew he was already no longer who he had just been.

The smell of blood coming from the heap on the highway aroused hunger in all of them. If they didn't clean the carcass, others would. Dinty Moore stepped forward, then hesitantly turned his head toward Brand X to be certain he was not about to usurp his leader's food. Kodak lunged toward Boyardee's carcass but jumped back as the headlights of an approaching car bore down. The car veered away from the furry mound. Dinty Moore licked his chops forlornly.

Brand X had thought of seizing the carcass and dragging it off behind his destination-ocotillo, but the car blurring past him convinced him that nothing was worth setting foot on that black highway for again. As if in confirmation of his decision, a Consolidated Freightways trailer truck roared past in the eastbound lane closest to him, and its outside row of tires, catching the shoulder, stung his face with a plume of gravel.

Brand X jumped back, pivoted, and broke out running, running headlong to get away from the broad black highway and to try to escape the horrible image, imbedded in him like a bristling clump of cholla, of the starved, brain-stunted little coyote who had followed him from home pinioned in an onslaught of light and struck down after he had already huddled in submission to it.

 **16**

A wounded Deer leaps highest—
I've heard the hunter tell—
'Tis but the Ecstasy of death—
And then the Brake is still!

EMILY DICKINSON, "A Wounded Deer"

A frontage road paralleled I-8 on the eastbound side for thirty miles out of Yuma. Brand X, fleeing the highway on which Boyardee lay dead, came to the frontage road where it had petered out to an unpaved, bulldozed swipe dead-ending at an illegal dump. The No DUMPING OF REFUSE sign, with the county ordinance number and penalties for disobedience cited on it, had served as no deterrent. The sign itself was bullet-riddled and nearly buried by the haphazard piles of garbage, cast-off furniture, broken appliances, and stripped-down car bodies surrounding it. The ground glittered with broken glass.

The coyotes fanned out to scavenge the mounds. They had never encountered such opulence. Albert and Hallie handled their garbage, what little there was of it, with great discretion to prevent its becoming a food source to scavengers meant to live off the land. Dinty Moore, Kraft, and Kodak had, on occasion, boldly nosed around among cans left strewn at hunters' cold campfires; but, when Brand X came on the dump, he was a virgin to garbage, and the rich, alluring smells emanating from the vast mounds of refuse enticed him to investigate. The garbage in the sealed plastic bags they ripped open was a rancid, mushy mulch, but the paper-bagged garbage, exposed to the desert air, was dried and crisp. Digging and strewing their way through pile after pile, mound after mound, they rapturously gorged on foods thoroughly exotic to them and ignored the banal rats and mice they would ordinarily have seized.

Kodak, his muzzle flecked with curds of cottage cheese, gobbled a slice of cantaloupe, rind and all. Chieko licked four cans of cat food and three jars of baby food meticulously clean. Kraft sampled french fries and the remains of a burrito. Salem polished off a cheesecake. Dinty Moore buried his muzzle in cans of spaghetti and pork and beans. Brand X pinned down an economy-size jar of peanut butter between his paws and snarled in frustration when his tongue couldn't reach the bottom.

Salem was strewing garbage from the outermost pile on the side of the dump which faced the frontage road when she noticed something amorphously floppy lying off by itself on the bare, glass-sharded ground. Intrigued by it, she approached it with her muzzle low and sniffed it. The fresh, human smell of it made her jump back with a strange, half-strangled yelp. It was a stuffed animal so thickly infused with the smell of the child who had held it close to her face and body that it smelled as if it were human itself.

At her yelp, the other coyotes' heads jerked up, and they dropped into crouches. From all sides, they crept out from behind rubbish piles that blocked Salem from view. Using her thunderstruck gaze as a compass, they looked in the direction it pointed, their muzzles extended and noses twitching but bodies fearfully hunched back into their hindquarters.

The dingy white object which Brand X saw did not seem to have merited such a yelp. Except for its soft-looking pliancy, it looked like a smooth, ordinary rock. He glanced at Salem for confirmation that this was indeed what had prompted her yelp. Her eyes, still baffled, blinked at it. He came forward and brusquely jammed his nose into the stuffed animal's worn plush. He leaped back as she had. But, emboldened by its inert neutrality, he was irresistibly drawn by the opportunity to quench his curiosity about the scent of two-leggeds. He thrust his muzzle into the pungent cloth to smell deeply the vivid human scent of its harmless shape.

Dinty Moore, Chieko, Kodak, and Kraft crowded forward to sniff it. Their heads snapped back, and they flicked astonished glances at one another before lowering their noses to smell once again the indubitably human scent this lifeless thing bore. Salem, watching them close in on her find, edged closer to it, her eyes fiercely covetous.

The noise from traffic on the highway obscured the sound of the pickup truck coming toward the dump on the frontage road. The plywood-sided bed of the truck, a Mexican gardener's battered old pickup, was piled high with twine-bound oleander cuttings. Crowning a dip, the headlights made a tableau of a circle of coyotes with lowered heads so tightly surrounding something that the driver could not see what it was.

"*Madre de Dios*," Vicente Escobar gasped, crossing himself.

He stomped on the brake pedal. The truck's rear end fishtailed, swinging it crosswise on the dirt road. Although the coyotes had been only momentarily caught in the headlights' glare, the image he had glimpsed stayed garishly illuminated in his mind's eye.

Vicente Escobar had seen the evening news on the Spanish channel, and the story about the missing, four-year-old girl had been on his mind as he drove to the dump. She was the same age as his little Sonia, and, like his Sonia, she had a stuffed Snoopy dog from which she was inseparable; and she had disappeared from Ligurta, a town just two miles from the dump.

Vicente flung open the door of the truck and ran toward the hunched, frozen coyotes. He took off his K-Mart cowboy hat as he ran and waved it wildly in the air, running and yelling in a horror-choked voice, "*Demonios! Demonios! Vayanse! Vayanse de aquí!*"

The strong, human scent in their noses from the stuffed animal combined with the terrifying sight of the noisy human with flailing arms coming at them, and the coyotes fled. Salem was the last to bolt. She ducked her head, seized the stuffed animal, and ran off with it dangling from her mouth like a pup.

Vicente knelt on all fours and sobbed in relief that it was not the child the coyotes had been surrounding after all. But the child must be here—or had been here. He had seen her Snoopy dog—unmistakable with its white body, black ears and spot, and big, dome-shaped head—hanging from the coyote's jaws.

Clutching in his fist the silver cross hanging around his neck, Vicente forced himself to search the dump for the child. He turned his truck to shine the headlights on the piles of refuse and shut off the engine to listen for her. His dread of finding the child dead made the dry, balmy night air through which he moved feel congealed, aqueously thick, resistant; his thudding heart, too big for his chest. He imagined himself having to wrap her little body in the grass-stained, oil-blotched canvas tarp reeking of gasoline from his lawn mower; he knew he could not do it. If—God forbid—she was dead, he would take off his shirt instead.

As he searched, he called out timidly to her in Spanish, telling her he was sorry he did not speak *inglés* but that he, too, had a *muchacha,* and he would take her home to her *madre* and *padre.* From the snapshot of her shown on television, he knew what she looked like; but he could not remember her name. He reviled himself as stupid that he couldn't.

He got in his truck, started the engine, and waited a minute in the hope that, not wanting to be left behind, she would suddenly dash out. All he saw were rats and mice.

Gripping the steering wheel in both hands and hunched so far forward that his cross clinked against the steering wheel, he drove two miles along the frontage road to Ligurta. As he drove, he kept seeing the way the coyotes had looked in his headlights, especially the one that had run off last with the missing child's Snoopy dog hanging from its mouth.

The nearest telephone was at the Texaco station. He stopped the truck next to its two pay phones. The station was closed. Since the interstate highway provided no access to Ligurta, there was no reason for a gas station to stay open until ten o'clock at night. He dialed the number for the Yuma County Sheriff's Station listed on the coin box. Calling the police frightened him. If they turned him over to Immigration, he would be deported.

The sound of the dispatcher's voice answering his call—that now there was someone he could tell about what he had seen and what he had feared he would find—unleashed a blurt of words from Vicente Escobar.

"What is your *name* and where are you *calling* from?" the dispatcher kept repeating.

"*Rápido! Rápido!*" Vicente shouted. "*Coyotes! Coyotes! La niña perdida estava en el basurero! Los coyotes la van a matar!*"

The only word the dispatcher could pick out was "*coyotes.*" Thinking the caller was using slang for the guides who smuggle illegal aliens across the Mexican border, he remembered the debacle a few years before when close to a hundred

men, women, and children from El Salvador had been abandoned by their *coyotes* and left to die in the searing, Arizona
desert, and he quickly transferred the call to Deputy
Armando Navarro.

Only then was the pay phone caller understood to be saying that he had seen the missing child's Snoopy dog at the
dump before it was carried off by a pack of coyotes—*"Sí, sí,
los animales, no hombres!"*—now roaming in the same area
where the little child must be.

Vicente Escobar's call unleashed the momentum of a jug-
gernaut waiting for a push. Two deputies were dispatched to
the Texaco station in Ligurta to take Vicente's statement. A
detective and four other deputies were sent to comb the
dump. A federal trapper and two county Animal Control officers were called in. The sheriff requested two helicopters
from the Laguna Army Air Field for civilian assistance. With
the two from the sheriff's department, that made a total of
four helicopters spotlight-scanning the desert for the child
and the alleged pack of coyotes.

Three four-wheel-drive Blazers from the sheriff's department, manned with deputies, Animal Control officers, and
S.W.A.T. sharpshooters, radiated out from the dump and
into the foothills of the Gila Mountains behind Ligurta to
coordinate with the helicopters in the ground-to-air team-
work system of aerial hunting which Jim Knapp, the federal
trapper, had recommended. Their main objective was to
find the child; but, in the meanwhile, on the theory that the
coyotes might attack the child if they happened on her, they
were going to locate and destroy the alleged pack.

A detective phoned Lorelei Spangler, the mother of the
missing child, to let her know that Jenny's Snoopy had been
seen at the dump outside Ligurta.

"Oh no, oh no, not there, not the *dump!*" she sobbed.

Lorelei Spangler was twenty-two years old. Jenny was her
middle child, sandwiched between a five-year-old boy and an

eighteen-month-old girl. Lorelei looked as if her youth had been broadsided by circumstances beyond her control. The spatter of adolescent pimples on her chin didn't tally with the dark circles under her eyes. She had tried to copy a hair style out of a magazine and had botched it. Her husband, a long-distance moving man, was on the road now, and she had not yet been able to reach him to tell him Jenny was missing. They lived in a flimsy, stucco house with sun-faded bedspreads stretched across the windows and a tangle of tricycles in the carport.

Yesterday Lorelei had repeatedly told Jenny to pick up her toys. Lorelei had finally gotten so mad that she had thrown Jenny's strewn toys into a garbage bag and taken them to the dump to teach Jenny a lesson. Later, feeling sorry about it and because Jenny was still so upset, she had taken her to the Yellow Front in Yuma and gotten her a new toy. But Jenny wouldn't play with it and had cried for her old ones.

Today, after lunch, Lorelei had put the baby and Jenny down for their naps, told the five-year-old to play in the house and not to go outside, and she, too, had taken a nap. When the baby woke up at three o'clock—waking Lorelei with her cries—Jenny was gone. The five-year-old had fallen asleep on the floor while watching television and hadn't seen her leave.

After frantically searching the neighborhood, Lorelei had called the police. It was when she heard herself giving the police a description of her child, the stuffed animal, and what she was wearing that it hit Lorelei that Jenny was truly gone.

Lorelei had not intentionally withheld from the police the story of throwing out Jenny's toys at the dump. It had not occurred to her—never once—that Jenny, only four years old, could have had the sense of direction, much less the stamina, to walk nearly three miles in blazing heat to the dump. Only when the detective told her that a Snoopy dog had been seen there did Lorelei realize what Jenny had done—gone to retrieve her thrown-out toys—and how truly heartbroken she must have been over them. It also meant that, now, wherever she was, Jenny was without her beloved "Noopy."

On the eleven o'clock local news, Paul Schroeder, the head of the U.S. Fish and Wildlife Service's Yuma office, was interviewed by telephone for his speculations as to whether a pack of coyotes would be likely to attack the child. He said that, first of all, because of the scarcity of the food supply in the desert, the desert coyote did not roam in packs but was an isolate, except during the breeding and denning season in winter and early spring.

Schroeder added that, curiously enough, however, two days ago he had received a call from Major Thurmond at the Yuma Proving Ground's Veterinary Health and Environmental Office regarding a suspicious "group" of seven apparently healthy coyotes that had been seen. Their location at the proving ground was some twenty-five miles from the dump, and, although it was by no means impossible for a coyote to cover such a distance, it was highly unlikely since a coyote's normal territorial range was ten to twelve miles at most.

Schroeder cited some extremely rare instances of lone coyotes attacking small children in residential canyons in Los Angeles County, but he explained that such urbanized coyotes had been conditioned to associate man with their food supply by well-meaning but uninformed people who fed them. Desert coyotes, he said, had a healthy and appropriate fear of mankind and avoided encounters with them.

When pressed as to whether this fear would extend to a four-year-old child, Schroeder said that as long as the child was alive and reasonably well, she would probably be safe from attack. When asked why, then, attempts were being made to locate and kill the coyotes seen at the dump, he cleared his throat and said, "Because I said *probably* safe."

Shortly before midnight, the spotlight on one of the

Blazers picked out Jenny's stuffed animal lying on open ground about four miles south of the dump. The sharpshooter on the passenger side jumped out. He prodded it with his shoe then squatted down by it. Pinching it up by the tip of the tail, he carried it, dangling, back to the vehicle.

"It's wet," he said. "How do you figure that?"

"Cause it's been in a coyote's mouth," the Animal Control officer said.

He aimed the spotlight down at the ground, got out of the Blazer, and pointed to the ground where faint impressions of paw prints could be seen in the hard, pinkish tan ground.

"Thing that worries me is, why would a little kid let go of something as loved-up-looking as this thing is? Seems to me like she'd be hanging onto it for dear life. Well, anyhow, since it's still wet, that's one coyote that can't be too far off."

"Yeah," the sharpshooter said, "you take a leak out here and the ground's dry before you get your fly zipped."

They turned off the Blazer's engine and sounded the siren. Coyote hunters had discovered that the wail of a siren inevitably made a coyote howl; and, once it howled, its location could be pinpointed.

They were raising their hands to cup their ears when the answering howls came. To untrained human ears, a lone coyote can sound like a chorus, but the Animal Control officer knew it really *was* a chorus, no doubt about it. He radioed the coyotes' location to the sheriff department's helicopter with Sgt. Hobson, a veteran of Vietnam choppers, piloting and Jim Knapp, the federal trapper, aboard.

Hobson brought the helicopter swooping in low, skimming over a skimpy line of mesquites along a dry wash. Jim Knapp was the best helicopter hunter around, but this was the first time he had ever been out at night doing this. He was skeptical about it being a pack—figured the Mexican at the dump probably had too much tequila under his belt and had been seeing at least double. An old trapper he had known called Scattershit used to say, "A coyote's the only animal on the face of the earth that can sound so lonesome but still like his own company best." Not that it mattered to Knapp. He was paid to destroy coyotes, and, day or night, a pack or a loner, he'd get the job done. He readied his 12-gauge shotgun at the cockpit window.

"There they are!" Knapp shouted. "Two, three, four— holy shit!—five of them! No, *six!*"

"Which one you want first?" Hobson said.

"I'll take the one that just ran down into the wash."

Hobson brought the helicopter parallel to the coyote running in the wash then slowed down to stay with it. He tried to train the spotlight on it, but the coyote kept zigzagging out of its illumination.

"Turn it off!" Knapp shouted. "There's enough moon."

A side wash coming down from the Gila Mountains joined the broad wash the coyote was in. Second-guessing what the coyote would do, Knapp fired the instant the coyote veered for it.

The force of the buckshot slamming into Kraft's body somersaulted him. For a few seconds he lay there with his legs—the three good ones and the stump of the fourth—still working as if he were running on a treadmill of air. His tongue lolled from his mouth. His ears flicked forward, his legs stopped their aerial running, and, drenched by the spotlight's sudden white glare, he died yearning for a brittlebush, a cactus, or a hole to shade himself from its intolerable brilliance.

"Got him!" Knapp shouted. "Let's take that one out there in front next. Must be the leader. We'll swing back and pick up this one later. It's not going anywhere."

Hobson turned off the spotlight and radioed the Blazer, "One down, five to go."

When the helicopter came in low over Brand X, its noise

was so domineering and all-encompassing it left nothing else in the world, not air for him to breathe nor ground for him to run over. It didn't spend itself in one profligate burst as had the enormous, intensely compacted explosion at the Yuma Proving Ground. Its terrifying pitch and intensity persisted: WHUMPwhumpWHUMPwhump.

Running headlong to escape it, unable to obtain the distance from it that would let him settle into the broadside trot he favored when threatened, Brand X strained toward the mountains with outstretched neck, reaching with his long muzzle for the haven of a mountain as he had reached for the ocotillo on the highway's far side. The airstream parted along the flying wedge of his head, flowed along his sides, and tapered off the rounded tip of his bushy tail. The helicopter following flexibly, effortlessly above him made him feel as if he had become like his father's white-eyed, decapitated head jutting from the front of the truck, lunging to outrace the very machine to which it was welded.

A cholla suddenly bristled before him. He veered to dodge it, and, at the moment of veering, his left shoulder burned with a searing, cauterizing pain. His left foreleg buckled, then his other legs also gave way, and he tumbled, rolling down the slope of the mountain he had barely gained, rolling and thinking he had not avoided the cholla in time after all and that now a chunk of it was deeply imbedded in his shoulder, piercing him with its excruciating, barbed, blonde thorns.

"Good shooting!" Hobson said.

"Nothin' to it," Knapp grinned. "Okay, let's go for the one that's cutting over to the carcass of the one we just got. Probably his mate."

Hobson radioed the Blazer, "Scratch one more. Four to go."

Knapp reloaded the shotgun and glanced over at Hobson

to see why he was keeping the helicopter hovering instead of getting onto the next coyote. He saw Hobson break out in a big smile as he listened to what was being said to him over his headphones.

"Great! Real lucky. Got you loud and clear," Hobson said and signed off. He turned to Knapp. "Party's over. They found the kid."

"Where abouts?"

"Sound asleep in a junk car about a half mile from the dump."

"She okay?"

Hobson laughed. "She will be once she gets that Snoopy dog of hers back. Had a whole mess of toys with her when they found her, but she's crying for her Snoopy. Good thing they found it down there. They're on their way to take it to her right now."

"You mean she ain't even *sunburned?*" Knapp said.

"Yeah, cooked about medium-rare. Pretty dehydrated, too, I guess. Lucky for her the windshield and all the windows on that old car was busted out or she would of roasted to death sleeping in there."

"Lucky and *then* some," Knapp said. He pulled the barrel of the shotgun in from the window, unloaded it, and held it upright with the butt of the stock on the floor between their seats. "Well, let's collect the two we got and bring 'em on in."

"Hey! Where'd it go?" Hobson said.

Knapp looked down from the hovering helicopter at the spot where the coyote had rolled to a stop. There was nothing there. "Well I'll be a son of bitch!" he said.

"Think maybe you just stunned it?"

"*You* saw the dive it took. It was a goner. Turn on your light there. We'll find it. Nowhere it can hide around here."

Knapp angled the empty shotgun across his knees and got out the .22 pistol which he used for finishing off coyotes at point-blank range on the ground.

Hobson swung the helicopter back and forth, swooped up and down, pulling close, drawing back, searching for the coyote that had started up the mountain's alluvial skirt—an elongated, moving target on an exposed slope—and had beyond question been shot; but it was nowhere to be seen. The spotlight illuminated only loose shale, some strewn boulders, a scattering of chollas and ocotillos, and the long, white ribs of a dead saguaro.

"Really bugs the hell outta me," Knapp said. "And the mate, how'd she manage to disappear into thin air, too? Gotta be a hole somewheres. I should of kept my eye on the bastard instead of getting sidetracked about the kid."

"Forget it. It's just another coyote you would of had to do paperwork on. Let's pick up that first one you got down in the wash and call it a night." Hobson switched off the spotlight and swung away from the slope. "Main thing is, the kid's been found."

Knapp edged a fingernail between his back teeth and worked out a bit of food, then he shook his head and grinned.

"Yeah," he said, "but I betcha once her folks get over being glad she's back they're sure gonna tan her hide."

17

You know my sitting down and my rising up;
you discern my thoughts from afar.
You trace my journeys and my resting-places
and are acquainted with all my ways.

PSALM 139

The helicopter's obliterating noise faded away until finally it was gone entirely, and Brand X was able to listen for small sounds to tell him where he was. He was not alone, that much he knew. There were others with him. He could feel their bodies crammed next to his, their legs and paws plaited with his. He tried to raise his head, but it scraped against rock.

The only other time in his life he had ever lain with others pressed tightly against him in the thick darkness of so thorough a shelter was when he had been a pup. Disoriented with shock and pain, he dazedly thought these must be his brothers and sisters pressed against him; comforted by the thought, he relaxed and let his mind start to drift away.

Suddenly, tall waves of panic rose up in him, making his sides heave, his heart bloat, his entrails twist within him as he understood the source of the excruciating pain in his shoulder. It was the rusty barbed wire, piercing him, pushing into him, seeking to get enough of him impaled on it to drag him out to where the two-legged squatted with the other end of the barbed wire in his gloved hand.

Brand X knew what was coming: first him, then the others, one by one skewered on the barbed wire, dragged out, writhing and whimpering, into the glare, then the rifle pushed against their heads and then the shot and then the gunnysack.

He cried out to the others to run, and, following his own command, his legs jerked with trying to, flailing against the bodies of the others and driving the agonizing wire still deeper into his shoulder. The hardness overhead crumpled his ears against his head as he struggled to get to his feet and flee. A moan dragged through his throat.

A nose softly touched his shoulder, then a tongue. The wire slipped out of him at the place where the tongue licked. Brand X went limp, subsiding. He lay perfectly still and let the tongue lick where the wire had gone in. The panic dissolved, fading like strong colors from an evening mountain, leaving cool shadows.

He knew now whose tongue was on his shoulder: the shy-eyed guardian of the jackrabbit haunch; the sister of the strange one. He lifted his head a little to look at her in the dark.

Her tongue paused, licked two more long strokes, then her nose gently nudged his head back down.

He felt another body wedged against him stir, as if whoever it was hoped to be recognized, too. But he was too exhausted to name that one. The nameless one sighed and settled again.

Lying on his side, he closed his eyes and felt the long, comforting strokes of Chieko's tongue pass over his fur, over the gunshot wound. He drowsily remembered the rocky promontory that had been his perch on the world and remembered the stone fish and the water tank by the mesquite tree. The memory of the water tank reminded him he was on a journey, and now he knew who else, beside Chieko, was there with him in the cramped shelter: the one whose pres-

ence was always close by. He raised his head slightly to ac-
knowledge him and felt Dinty Moore's tail thump eagerly
against him.

Having identified who was with him, he realized where he
must be and how he must have gotten there. After he had
dodged the cholla and tumbled down the mountain, he had
come to a stop against a boulder. Chieko had reached him
first, then Dinty Moore had come. He remembered the
helicopter hanging eternally above him like a red-tailed hawk
about to dive onto a hapless rabbit.

He understood what Chieko and Dinty Moore must then
have done by recalling the thread-waisted wasp he had idly
watched his last day on home ground as it had dragged the
caterpillar it had killed down its hole: the tugging, jux-
tapositioning, straddling, angling, inching of it, and, finally,
the wasp itself going down the hole and pulling the caterpillar down on top of itself. The picture in his mind of Dinty
Moore and Chieko desperately dragging him, an inert bur-
den, around the boulder to an abandoned den beneath the
boulder's downhill side and getting him in it by pulling him
and crowding in with him made him stir as if to shift his
cramped limbs, but it was the overwhelming weight of
gratitude on his heart he sought to ease.

Throughout the nights that followed, Chieko hunted for
two. She herself ate meagerly in order to bring Brand X
mice, pocket gophers, lizards, cottontails, ground squirrels,
and, once, a jackrabbit. Sometimes she brought them to him
whole; sometimes she regurgitated them for him like a
mother for her pups. After leaving the food near him, she
would go off a short way and lie down. If he did not immediately eat, she would get up, sniff the food to be sure there was
nothing wrong with it, nudge it still closer to him, then go
back and lie down.

She would have carried water to him in her mouth, but her

jaws did not know how to hold it. She thought of Salem's wastefully dripping teats but knew Brand X would not suckle from her.

When he let her, she licked the wound in his shoulder, and he saw her eyes thronged with sorrow for his pain. When he limped out from the hole beneath the boulder to defecate or pass water, she watched him with a solicitous, encouraging eye. She studied him closely for signs of improvement and rejoiced at his slightest gain in mobility.

The first time he hazarded a hobbling trot Chieko saw not the awkwardness of it but his effort at it. When the leg under the wounded shoulder gave way after a few steps and he fell, she whined so sharply for his pain that Brand X's head jerked toward her, thinking she had been hurt.

While maintaining the pretense of aloofness, he spent long stretches of time covertly observing her. Having known only himself well and truly, he now came to know another. He noticed the specifically particular look of her: the diamond of short, buff-colored fur that began between her eyes, fanned out across her muzzle, and ended in a point at her nose; the dark stripes wrapping around her sides like ribs; the creamy fur of her eyebrows that was less dense than others', lending a more open, unfurrowed expression to her golden brown eyes. There was a freshness, a poignance, a dearness about her face that registered on him profoundly.

He thought her face looked *informed,* not merely about matters of survival but about matters of the spirit. Looking at her filled him with a sense of harmony, yet also made him feel unfulfilled somewhere within himself.

Because Brand X, if left alone, would have been no more able than a gangly pup to adequately defend himself, Chieko and Dinty Moore hunted in shifts as coyote parents do. One night Chieko's turn to hunt came while Brand X was sleeping, and he awoke to find her gone. The unexpected vacancy of her customary spot so jolted him that he hobbled over to it just to smell her reassuring scent-shape on the ground. That night, she noticed his tail thumped the ground when she returned. She, however, took it as a sign of welcome to the squirrel in her jaws rather than the welcome sight of herself.

Dinty Moore came and went. A great one for bustling about and keeping tabs on things, he would usually come trotting back to the boulder with a grin spread over his face and his eyes eager to share what they had seen. As devotedly as Chieko brought him food, Dinty Moore brought Brand X good cheer and the kind of news a child coming in from winter play brings in his pink cheeks, runny nose, and the cold, fresh air on his bundled clothes. As Chieko became Brand X's missing link to himself, Dinty Moore became his link to the world his gunshot wound prevented him from exploring and to the ancestral coyote world which, as an orphan, he had missed out on. They lent spaciousness to the confines of his convalescence.

With Brand X crippled, Kodak's inflated sense of superiority now had free rein. He watched from afar the comings and goings of Chieko and Dinty Moore from the boulder where Brand X lay, and he gloated at the sight of Brand X pathetically hobbling about.

Chieko had encountered Salem the first time she had left Brand X to hunt food for him. When Salem had fled from the helicopter, she had become separated from Brand X. She had been crisscrossing the mountains for hours since, trying to pick up his trail, when she had spotted Chieko and approached her. They had exchanged stiff-legged, formal sniffs; and Salem had smelled Brand X on her sister's fur. Dinty Moore's scent was also on her from the night before, when the three of them had lain entwined in the crowded den, but Salem had noticed only that of Brand X.

Believing she had lost Brand X to Chieko, Salem had

arched her back and, with a gape of teeth, scuttled sideways at her like a scorpion. Chieko had run away, her fur prickling with fear. From then on, she had gone out of her way to avoid Salem.

But the dawn came when Chieko was returning to the boulder with a kangaroo rat in her jaws for Brand X, and Salem and Kodak, spontaneously teaming up, trailed her. There was nothing she could do, no way she could stop them.

With Chieko out hunting, it had been Dinty Moore's turn to remain with Brand X. When he saw Salem and Kodak following Chieko as she came up the slope, he leaped to his feet and his chest rumbled warnings. Brand X, lying crosswise in front of the boulder, raised his head from his paws and looked downhill at them but did not stand. He knew that for Kodak to see him wobble would only boost his newfound sense of superiority and encourage him to a confrontation which Brand X could ill afford.

Chieko came to where Brand X lay and dropped the kangaroo rat. Her downcast eyes murmured abject apology for having led them to him. She lay down beside him on his injured side, hiding his wound from view. She had never presumed to lie closely side by side with him like this before.

Kodak and Salem crowded together beside a saguaro as if in need of a column of shade to shield them from the seething sun. But the sun had not yet risen; it was only faintly bleaching the eastern sky. Salem threw a glance at Brand X and Chieko, then whirled to attend to an itch at the base of her tail, snapping at her fur and frantically nibbling down through it, the urgency of the itch proportionate to her inability to bear the sight of her sister lying beside Brand X.

Kodak's lip flexed into a snarl, and he eyed Brand X as if contemptuously assessing just how soon he would be carrion for vultures. Brand X looked steadily back at him. Unable to withstand the intensity of his gaze, Kodak shifted his eyes to Chieko lying next to him, then glanced at Dinty Moore standing off to the side.

He stepped forward and, with a gloating grin, began to pace about smugly like an arrogant orator warming to his subject. Trotting briskly back and forth, he lorded his strength and fitness over the incapacitated Brand X.

But, finding he had to slit his eyes against the golden glare of Brand X's inexorable gaze, Kodak began to have doubts. Perhaps Brand X was like a healthy bird who drags a wing to trick an enemy into thinking it is easy prey. Perhaps, despite the kangaroo rat she had brought him, Chieko had not merely been out hunting. Perhaps she had been sent by Brand X to lure him into following her back to him so that he, once again sound of body, could punish his mutinous lack of respect by suddenly springing up at him, throwing him onto his back, and lunging for his throat. One thing was certain: with Brand X, there was no telling, there was no fathoming him.

As Kodak's misgivings burgeoned, the strut went out of his pacing. It now took on an urgent, furtive objective: to steal a look at Brand X's wound; to size up the fitness of an adversary who might at any moment spring at him.

Brand X lay with his chest held high, his head raised, and his legs parallel in front. Chieko was lying so close beside him that the outer guard hairs on their shoulders touched. No matter what angle he took, Kodak could detect no injury on Brand X.

Salem ceased trying to get at the maddening itch and stood with her tail hanging lifelessly against her hind legs and her head lowered as if in exhaustion. Her eyes scalded with jealousy as she took in Chieko lying shoulder to shoulder with Brand X. Her lip skinned back from her teeth, and her head craned forward.

Chieko looked at her sister's blazing eyes and futile teats, and a lifetime of docility was swept aside by a surge of rage at her sister's ill will. Her muscles gathered to send her springing at Salem's throat.

Feeling her body tighten against his, Brand X swung his head to look at her; and she remembered, just in time, that she could not leave his side. If she sprang at her sister, his wound would be revealed to Kodak. She did all that was left for her to do: she went for Salem's throat by springing straight into her eyes.

The look which she sent deep into Salem's eyes issued forth from the intimacy of her history with her, a dense backlog of pent-up contempt, long-suffering patience, and swallowed wrath. It was a look which said she would pity any pups ever born from her, would rejoice when her path ended, and that, when it ended, neither she nor any other worthy moon-caller would sing farewell to her spirit.

Blasted by her sister's condemning gaze, Salem shrank back into her haunches and pawed at her stunned eyes.

Brand X maintained the high carriage of his head and chest as he glared at Kodak with a deep, banishing frown. Kodak abandoned the last of his remaining bravado and rounded on Salem as if it were all her fault. Snarling at her, he shot her a glance so menacing that it startled the hard glitter out of her eyes. He shouldered her in a rough command to follow him, then, without waiting to see if she obeyed, ran down the mountain without a backward glance.

Salem stood stock-still in the first sunlight buttering the slope. Brand X slumped over onto his side, toppling as if a keystone had been yanked out of an arch, and she saw that not only was he wounded but that the pain he had endured to hide it—keeping his chest and head erect and his eyes fiercely battle-ready—had been monumental. Seeing the wound, Salem understood why Chieko had lain close beside him and

that, in order to protect him, her sister had forsaken the longing of her teeth to destroy her.

As the outcome of events and the finality of the moment
bore down on her, crushing her illusions and turning her
hopes rancid, Salem saw that she and Kodak had not been
tricked or bluffed or outsmarted by Brand X and Chieko.
They had been vanquished by their betters.

Tail lowered, head lowered, eyes lowered, she slunk off in
belated obedience to Kodak's command.

 18

The Editor
The Yuma Courier
Yuma, Arizona

Dear Mr. Editor,

Back two weeks ago your front page had side-by-side pictures showing a lost child that got found and a trapper dangling a dead coyote upside down by his tail. I have studied those pictures the same way I used to study passages in the Bible that had me confused about their meaning, but how you got coyotes mixed in with that little child being lost is still beyond *me!* Your own story says that all those coyotes did was raid a dump! It seems like folks want to blame coyotes for everything but the weather.

What's more, that dead coyote was one that used to come every day to drink from our tank before we had to cap our well because of copper mine tailings. It's not just his being three-legged that lets me know it's him that trapper is holding up. I've seen plenty others with stumps like his. It's that *pack* nonsense your paper talked about.

That trapper said he counted six coyotes in all, and we've been missing seven of ours recently. (The seventh one was a pitiful little thing that must of died or got himself killed somewhere between here and that dump.) Those seven of ours were no pack though. No sir, they were one-by-ones just like all the coyotes out here are, except during their family time of year.

Now here's what I want to say. Coyotes may just be varmints to you, but to me they were the best neighbors a body could ask for.

I thank you for the time you have spent reading this old woman's angry letter. I felt like I just had to get this off my chest and put in a good word for the coyotes. Maybe our Maker—the coyotes' and mine, I'm meaning—will think I have put this pencil to good use, too.

Sincerely,
Hallie Durham Ryder

19

A survey of the desert scene soon produces in an observer a vigorous recoil from the notion of Nature as mother.

ROSS CALVIN, *Sky Determines*

It was the fence Brand X came to one night while out hunting that urged him to resume his journey. For days now he had refused the food which Chieko brought so that hunger would force him to use the leg that wanted to dangle from his gunshot shoulder.

The moon had rounded out, showing the pale gray lizard splayed across its fullness like a continent, and it inclined Brand X to venture farther than he had on previous nights. As he limped along the broad wash in which Kraft had been shot, he came to a barbed wire fence. The fence was bloated outward by a tangle of branches, sticks, rocks, and uprooted bushes which had caught and mounded against the leaning fenceposts and lower strands when the wash had been running hard.

Until he encountered the fence, he had not known if his legs should still be asked to carry his embodied spirit to Skywater. He had thought perhaps his spirit would have to make the journey alone. But the fence—because it was there, because it stood across the dry water-trail that was the path to Skywater—inflamed him with resolution to continue the journey.

He called out to Chieko and Dinty Moore who were hunting separately. His summons brought them running to him with such concern on their faces that he realized they had feared for him. When they saw him sitting by the fence and in no apparent danger, they eyed him inquisitively.

Brand X stood and began to nose aside the debris clogged against the lowest strand of the barbed wire fence. When it was cleared, he tentatively pawed the sandy ground under the bottom strand as if testing its ability to be dug, then he started digging. Chieko glanced at Dinty Moore with confusion and alarm. The look Dinty Moore returned shrugged off her worry and told her to let him be.

But she could not bear to see the way the foreleg beneath the wounded shoulder fumbled at the ground, struggling to alternate with the other leg's digging. She rushed forward and swung her hindquarters against Brand X's body to crowd him away from the hole, and she began to dig frantically at it on his behalf. He moved away from the sand flying between her hind legs. She turned her head to check his expression, fearing she had overstepped in pushing him away. He took her muzzle gently in his jaws and waggled it back and forth. She bowed her head, bashful with happiness at this gesture of affection.

After he released her muzzle, she fell to digging again, and, as he watched her, he thought about her influence on him, how she influenced him the way wind influences a tree, drawing out its resilience, testing its resistance, teaching the tree things about itself it would not have known if the wind had not stirred it, weathered it, gently teased it, and sung through it. Dinty Moore could enlighten him, but only Chieko could make him feel enlarged.

Using the hole she had dug under the barbed wire's bottom strand, Brand X bellied under the fence and, in doing so, resumed the journey to Skywater. He was once again following the trail that water had taken when it, too, had tried to reach Skywater; and of those who had begun the journey with him, it had come down to only these two—Chieko and Dinty Moore—who were still with him.

At the tail end of the Gila Mountains, Brand X turned west to follow a dry water-trail out toward the towering Algodones Dunes of the Yuma Desert: sun-dazed, barren, wind-rippled, peaked dunes of sand the pale, strawy tan of coyote pups' fuzz. The elegant sculpture of the dunes had a mathematical purity in the trigonometry of its shadows, the plane geometry of its bare masses. It was desert reduced to unembellished essence, land which proclaimed itself the antithesis of water, partaking of so little water that, paradoxically, its sand resembled water, the tidal waves of the dunes rippled like wind-stirred water.

Deep within himself, Brand X had known that the last land before the endless water of Skywater would be sand-water. It was as if he had unknowingly carried a map of it folded in his mind, and now, unfurling it and overlaying the actual terrain onto his mental map, he found they coincided perfectly.

But to Chieko and Dinty Moore the sight of the looming sand dunes was so daunting that they could not keep themselves from exchanging repeated glances of astounded dread at the direction Brand X had chosen to take. Their heavy-hearted gazes recoiled from a landscape that lit his with reckless euphoria.

The dry wash which had turned Brand X toward the dunes disappeared at the onset of the dunes. Throughout his journey he had heeded his instinct to always follow the downhill trail that water had made in trying to reach Skywater. Now, for the first time, there was no dry water-trail to follow. Before, instinct had shown him the way. Now he listened for his spirit to show it to him. Its voice was softer, its meaning harder to catch, and he had to stop often to listen for its counsel.

At a pace dictated by his wound, Brand X led Dinty Moore and Chieko. They climbed up sand-hollowed cuts on the gentler slopes of the dunes' windward side, then plunged down the abrupt dropoffs of the dunes' wind-shadowed leeward side. They discovered that the dunes' lower slopes had better footing because the sand was coarser; but the fine sand deposited near the top of the dunes by lighter winds made them sink in up to their chests.

A few creosote bushes, white bursage, buckwheat, Mormon tea, and four-wing saltbush sprawled on the dunes from roots buried deep in the hollows between dunes. Shorn of their foliage by sandblasting winds, their gangly height reflected a constant, desperate effort to keep from being buried alive. The delicate calligraphy of claw, paw, bird, and insect tracks imprinted in the sand informed Brand X, Chieko, and Dinty Moore that life—and therefore food—was to be had even here. They saw the tracks of deer mice, kangaroo rats, sand crickets, weevils, roadrunners, Gambel quail, fringe-toed lizards, kit foxes, and sidewinders.

Dinty Moore scared up a horned lizard among some tangled strands of wind-blown buckwheat. When he lunged to catch it, it squirted him in the face with a hiss of blood spurted from its eyes. Dinty Moore leaped back, startled out of his wits to find himself bloodied in such a manner; and the lizard escaped.

Dinty Moore swiped at his face with his paw, then knelt in the sand with his hindquarters in the air and rubbed his muzzle from side to side to rid himself of the humiliating blood. Dinty Moore, who had always loved a good joke,

whether on himself or another, failed to find anything hu-
morous in the horned lizard's act of self-defense. His cheer-
ful good nature had finally failed him. For the rest of the
night, as he slogged up and down the dunes, Dinty Moore's
mind kept harping on what a low-down, disgusting trick the
horned lizard had played on him.

The dunes put Chieko's kind nature to its severest test,
too. Trudging cumbrously through their sands, she had to
censor her eye from judgment, her mouth from whimpering
complaint, and her mind from berating Brand X's decision.
She shrouded herself in silence. She watched his limp
worsen and the leg draw up under the injured shoulder, and
she censored herself deeper and deeper into silence.

By dawn they had crossed the five-mile width of the Algodones Dunes. The sand levelled off, and a fence was in
sight. Since the creosote bushes on the other side of the sand-
drifted fence looked as miserably spindly as those close by,
Brand X collapsed in exhaustion under one where he was,
and Dinty Moore and Chieko sought shelter under others
nearby.

As the sun climbed the sky, the bushes' overlapping
shadows retreated, leaving Brand X, Chieko, and Dinty
Moore sun-stranded in panting isolation under their three
small islands of shade in a sea of scalding sand.

They slept. They dozed. They snapped at flies. They cir-
cumnavigated their bushes to stay within the shifting, sun-
pierced shade. As the sun gained its zenith and devoured
their crucial shade, they pushed close against the center of
their bushes. Dinty Moore could not stop thinking about the
horned lizard that had squirted blood from its eyes. Chieko
stayed wrapped within her silence. Brand X monitored the
pain in his shoulder and, through slitted eyes, studied the
granular, glaring white terrain that jiggled with heat.

The sun finally slid down the sky, and once again the

elongated shadows of their three bushes overlapped and merged. Ravenous for food, water, and an end to this sandwater land, they came out from under their bushes. They were approaching the fence when a scent reached them. Brand X stopped, raised his head high, and with small jerks of his muzzle sniffed the air. Chieko tilted her muzzle skyward and stood poised with her nostrils flaring. Dinty Moore craned his neck and bobbed his head to catch the intriguing scent. Its pungent, aromatic complexity made it provocatively attractive. Exchanging puzzled looks, the three of them started toward it as if spellbound.

Because Brand X's shoulder had stiffened up badly during the hours of inactivity, reducing him to an awkward hobble, and because Dinty Moore paused to snatch a gecko that darted past, Chieko was the first to belly under the fence and eagerly lower her nose to the alluring scent; and so it was her leg on which the scent-baited trap snapped its steel jaws.

She did not cry out. It was as if her self-imposed censorship and long-sustained silence in the dunes had been the preparation for this deepest silence of all, the silence of the captive. Rearing back violently, she was yanked by the short chain that went from the trap to the buried peg and thrown down hard onto her side.

Brand X and Dinty Moore saw her thrashing, then saw the steel jaws biting her leg about three inches up from her paw. Dinty Moore leaped forward as if seconds mattered. But Brand X stood where he was, and it was not the imbalance of standing on three legs that made him sway unsteadily.

It was Chieko clamping him with her eyes as tightly as the trap clamped her leg, clamping her eyes, raucous with silence, on him as she lowered her muzzle to her trapped leg to pay the price for her exuberant curiosity about the alluring scent. Clamping his eyes with hers, she lowered her head to set about the grisly task of gnawing off her own leg: the exorbitant price for priceless freedom.

20

. . . in the way wherein I walk
they have hidden a trap for me.
Listen to my cry for help,
for I have been brought very low;
save me from those who pursue me,
for they are too strong for me.

PSALM 142

Ray Draper checked the colors of the sunset and figured he had less than an hour of light left to finish making the rounds of his traps. The pickup slewed in and out of the sandy road's ruts as he chugalugged the last of his beer, crumpled the can, and tossed it out the window. Lifting the unsnapped flap of his cowboy shirt pocket, he took out his cigarettes. He squeezed the pack and felt four. He banged the steering wheel with the heel of his hand; the way he smoked, that wouldn't hold him, and by now he was a good fifteen miles from the nearest place to buy more.

Both Draper and his truck looked much older than they were. The Chevy pickup was only eight years old, but its green paint had been sandblasted off by the hard, gritty winds of the Yuma Desert; the windshield was so pitted from sandstorms that when he drove toward a setting sun he might as well have been driving blindfolded, and in the middle of the windshield there was a big cobweb of smashed glass where a rock had hit.

Draper was forty-two but looked sixty. His leathery face was troughed and furrowed with overlapping, garbled lines; his small eyes were out of kilter and pouchy. He usually had several days' stubble since he only shaved when he wasn't too hungover to make it risky. His long-lobed ears stuck straight out from the sides of his head like a badger's. His hair was thinning out on top; to hide it he always wore his beat-up old Stetson with the brim that curled up like a sole separated from a shoe.

Draper's father had been a miner up in Jerome, Arizona, until the copper played out, leaving Jerome a ghost town. Ray Draper had become a coyote trapper because it was outdoor work and there was no danger of the open range running out of coyotes the way the Little Daisy Mine had run out of copper.

Hungover as he was, Draper hadn't felt like checking his line of traps today, but a few afternoon beers had helped, and he had to admit he had gotten off to a good start. The first trap, east of the dunes near Vopoki Ridge, had had one in it, a dead bitch. Nothing made him madder than finding some googly-eyed ringtail cat or a three-pound kit fox in a trap meant for coyotes. Nothing, that is, except finding just a coyote's paw attached to a chewed-off leg in a sprung trap.

"Now a rabbit's foot, that's good luck, but a coyote's foot, that's my hard luck," he liked to say.

From the look of the one in that first trap, he figured she must have sprung it soon after he had set it three days ago. The trapped leg had swollen to five times normal size before she had finally died of thirst and the sun's full brunt beating down on her. She was so bloated from lying dead in the sun for another day that she had looked as if she was about to explode.

He had heard about some new regulations saying traps had to be visited daily so as not to prolong the suffering of the captive animal and that trap jaws were supposed to be burlap-wrapped to keep the steel from biting into the leg, but he wasn't about to let a bunch of squeamish bleeding hearts back in Washington, D.C. cramp his style.

After he had shooed the vultures off, he had been surprised to see the trapped coyote had the teats of a whelping bitch on her. He had never seen such a thing in September. A coyote bitch didn't even come into heat until January. From the tracks, he knew there had been another coyote with her, and from the wider stance and deeper impression of the tracks he could tell it had been a male.

The story their paw prints told had read like a primer to Draper: See the two coyotes trotting along. See them scent the bait and turn toward the trap. See the bitch get caught in it. See her roil up the sand, lunging and whirling and jerking around. See the male run away.

Heading toward the next trap, with the dead bitch gunnysacked in the bed of the pickup, Draper tore another can of Coors out of the cardboard six-pack on the seat and, holding it between his thighs, popped the tab. The truck hit a bump, sloshing beer on him. He yowled at its coldness and pinched the crotch of his jeans away from himself, muttering curses and feeling like a martyr for making the round of his traps while he wanted to be on a barstool at the Sixshooter Saloon in Yuma.

Straining to see into the failing light through the sand-pitted windshield, he looked to see if there was anything in the trap he had set right up next to the barbed-wire fence at the dunes' western end; and what he thought he saw but could not believe he was seeing made him forget about the spilled beer, his cigarette shortage, and the Sixshooter.

"Giddyup!" he said to his truck. "Three of 'em!"

Berserk with terror at the oncoming truck, Chieko stopped biting her trapped leg and bit at the trap, dug frantically at the ground with her free foreleg, and thrashed so violently she was somersaulted onto her back when the chain jerked her up short. Brand X darted in to nudge and poke her, urging her to redouble her efforts to free herself. Dinty Moore paced agitatedly, glancing from her to the truck bearing down on them.

"Stay put, stay put, stay put," Draper intoned with fervent intensity.

He pulled excitedly at a flap of chapped skin on his bottom lip as he formulated a plan. As soon as he got in range, he would stop the truck and shoot the two loose ones. Luckily, one of them was gimpy. He'd take it last, the other one first. Then he'd chloroform the one in the trap to keep as a replacement for the bitch that had died last week.

Draper took great pride in the powerful allure of the urine-based mashes of coyote anal glands, jackrabbit and rattlesnake flesh, and dashes of fish oil he concocted as bait for his traps. That was why he liked to keep a coyote or two caged up at his place, and sometimes, in spring, after dousing the rest of the litter with kerosene and tossing a match into the den, he brought home a pup. He usually collected the captive coyotes' urine in a round depression in a corner of their small, filthy, sloping-floored cage; but occasionally he just tied a cord tightly around the captive coyote's penis—or, if it was a bitch, sewed the vulva shut—and forced quantities of water down the coyote's gullet, then, after letting it stew a couple of days, killed the coyote, cut out its bladder, and collected the urine that way.

Since it had been three days ago he had set the traps, he hadn't expected to find a live one in any of them, but from the way she was fighting the trap, he could tell this one was fresh-caught. If she'd been out there all day, the sun would have taken the spunk out of her in no time.

He eased the truck to a stop, turned off the engine, and

took down his varmint rifle from the gunrack mounted across the rear window. He popped open the glove compartment to get out ammunition. Crammed-in junk burst out, spilling onto the glove compartment door and down onto the rubber floor mat. The corner of his mouth twitched with tension as he rooted through the remaining contents of the glove compartment: matchbooks, a lone White Mule work glove, a small brown bottle of iodine, three rusty padlocks, a stick of spearmint gum as hard as a rock, some pornographic Mexican postcards, a tin of Bufferin, greasy shop rags, a bolo tie with a chunk of turquoise, and sloppily refolded road maps.

Spotting the red end-flap of a Remington box way at the back, he yanked it out, then, suspicious of its lightness, shook it hard: empty. He crumpled it and hurled it out the window and bemoaned his bad habit of keeping several boxes of ammunition going at the same time instead of starting one box and using it until it was empty.

"Come *on,* come *on,* come *on,*" he muttered furiously. "They're not going to wait around all night."

Sprawling across the seat to go through the pile that had fallen onto the floor mat, he banged his head on the sharp corner of the glove compartment door. He slammed it shut in fury. The door popped back open. He slammed it again. Again, it fell open. He banged the door back and forth then drew up his legs and kicked it shut. It fell back open. He yelled obscenities.

Doubling over, he rummaged under the seat, pulling out take-out food containers, wadded paper napkins, plastic spoons, tiny corrugated paper squares of salt and pepper, and shreds of dried cole slaw. "*Hold* the cole slaw, *no* cole slaw," he always said at the drive-up window, but they were forever sticking it in the bag with the rest of the order anyway.

He touched a likely feeling cardboard box and, hope surging, pulled it out. It was a Remington box, and it had bullets in it; but the bullets were for his .22 pistol, which he had left on the kitchen table for cleaning but hadn't gotten around to doing.

He tipped his hat back on his head, crossed his arms on the steering wheel, laid his stubbled chin on his arms, and stared out the pitted windshield at the three coyotes.

"*Now* what, asshole," he said.

Chloroform, that's what, he thought. Knock out the bitch in the trap, stuff her in a gunnysack, and the hell with the other two. He dug around in the pile under the open glove compartment door, not about to try again to get it to stay shut. He had seen the chloroform when he had been looking for the ammunition. He found it: a dented metal can with a skull and crossbones on the torn label.

Draper got out of the truck, expecting the two loose coyotes to finally take off. But no. Eager to flee but not giving in to it, Dinty Moore's forelegs ran in place, and, while Chieko thrashed her hindquarters wildly from side to side, Brand X began digging frantically at the place where the short chain was connected to the buried stake of the trap.

"Hey!" Draper yelled. "Oh no you don't!"

Sticking the chloroform can in his armpit, Draper grabbed his canvas tarp, work gloves, and chloroform rag from the back of the truck and ran toward them. He knew firsthand of coyotes in traps that had dug up the stake and, holding the chain in their teeth so as not to trip over it, dragged themselves off, trap, chain, stake, the whole shebang. He wasn't about to lose a perfectly good trap—and the coyote in it—that way.

As he bore down on them, Chieko leaped back so hard she was thrown to the ground. She stumbled to her feet and leaped again and again was thrown down. Brand X and Dinty Moore backed off, their hackles standing with fear and their lips twitching back as they peered at him through thick layers of terror; but they didn't bolt.

Draper took off his hat and waved it at them, humiliated to find himself trying to shoo off coyotes, his livelihood. He was beginning to wonder what was wrong with them, what was making them so bold, why, when only one of them could be her mate, they both refused to take off. Suddenly he thought he knew. *They see I don't have a gun!* Infuriated to think they were mocking his incompetence, he shouted, "I'll wipe those grins off your ugly faces!"

He flung down the tarp, the rag, the gloves, and the chloroform can and, grabbing a rock, hurled it at them. It hit Dinty Moore's ribs. He yipped, wheeled, and ran off fifty yards then stopped and turned. Draper leaned over for another rock. Brand X retreated at a lame lope to where Dinty Moore stood.

"Fast learner, huh," Draper snarled, throwing the rock. It fell short.

He put on the work gloves, unscrewed the cap on the chloroform, and tipped the can against the rag. A thin line of chloroform trickled out. In utter disbelief, Draper upended the can and shook it over the rag. Five drops dripped out. He yanked off one of the gloves and threw it down on the ground.

"Aw, Jesus, come *on!*"

He shook the can furiously and banged the bottom of it with the heel of his hand. Rearing back, he heaved the empty can at Brand X and Dinty Moore. They jumped back as it clattered in front of them. He swiped up his glove from the ground and, jamming his fingers into it, strode toward Chieko as if she were the cause of all his troubles. She plunged and leaped, twisting her body and biting at the trap and her own leg in it.

With a quick movement of his wrist, he flung the tarp over

her head when she reared back from him to the tautest extent of the chain, then, straddling her and squeezing her sides between his bent knees, he jammed the pungent rag into the opening he had left in the tarp and hoped like hell there was enough chloroform on it to get the job done. He gripped her until he felt the fight go out of her, until she became watery, then he opened his knees, and she slumped over onto his boot. He looked around for the gunnysack and realized he had forgotten to get it when he had gotten the tarp, the gloves, and the rag. He went back to the pickup, found one crumpled under a jerry can and, shaking it out, returned to her.

Seeing the gunnysack swinging from Draper's gloved fist, Brand X went rigid. When Draper had thrown the tarp over Chieko's head, gripped her from behind like a grotesque mate, and done something to her that had made her topple and fall over when he let go of her, he had watched with dazed incomprehension, like a child witnessing an act he knows is wrong but lacks the knowledge to know why. But Brand X knew why gunnysacks were wrong; they robbed him of what was precious to him: his brothers and sisters, the good water-place, and now her. His gaze cauterized to the gunnysack, he watched Draper carry it to where Chieko lay splayed on the ground and drop it beside her head.

Draper opened the jaws of the trap, releasing her swollen, chewed-up leg. He congratulated himself for having gotten there in time to find her still attached to it. He prodded her with his boot tip: knocked out all right. He stuffed her into the gunnysack, knotted the top, and carried her—light little thing, twenty, twenty-two pounds—to the pickup where he slung her up and over the tailgate and dropped her. She landed next to the other gunnysacked bitch, the bloated, stinking one with the out-of-season teats.

Brand X had watched the mouth of the gunnysack open

wide and swallow Chieko whole. Watched it bulge with her as it had bulged with his brothers and sisters and as it had bulged with droppings to ruin the good water-place. Watched the gunnysack that had devoured her be thrown into the back of a truck as his brothers and sisters had been. Brand X threw back his head and closed his eyes and cried out.

"Howlin' for your missus, huh," Draper laughed, turning as he got into the truck, one boot on the ridged metal doorsill. "Well, tough shit, pal! I got her now!"

Draper swung the truck around, calling it a day because it was almost night, he was down to two cigarettes and one beer, and out of chloroform, the right bullets, and luck. He glanced into the rearview mirror to take a goodbye-and-good-riddance look at the place where he had so thoroughly messed up; and he saw the two coyotes chasing him down the jeep trail, running in his tire tracks, one in each rut, eating his dust, the gimpy one lagging behind.

"I'll be a son of a bitch if they're not *followin'* me!" he said.

On a whim, he stopped the truck, got out, and dropped the tailgate, just to make the invitation crystal clear, because, being only barely knee-high to him, they might not be able to jump up over a raised tailgate. Stepping aside, he took off his beat-up old cowboy hat and made a sweeping bow with it, then he climbed into the cab of the truck and swung himself around on the seat so he could see out the rear window through the gunrack.

Dinty Moore held himself in check until Brand X pulled up even with him, then they loped side by side. They had lost so much ground to the truck that Dinty Moore knew they would never be able to stay with it at Brand X's wounded rate. When the truck suddenly stopped, he saw his moment to act on Brand X's behalf. Saw it had fallen to him to carry out Brand X's urgent but futile intention to stay with Chieko, to abide by her as she had with him when he was shot. Saw, with unutterable reluctance, that his loyalty to Brand X required him to leave Brand X behind. He swung his head and gave Brand X a farewell look of pure devotion, then he lengthened his stride and pulled ahead of Brand X to take advantage of the truck's halt.

Dinty Moore was running flat-out when he reached the back of the truck and, without breaking stride, sprang and came down with his claws sliding in the metal grooves of the bed. He sprawled hard against the gunnysack with Chieko inside it. He felt her slow breath push through the woven burlap, and he smelled the sickening sweet chloroform fumes on her muzzle. The truck leaped forward, and he slid backward toward the lowered tailgate.

"Goddamn, it *worked!*" Draper said. Flooring it, he sent up roostertails of dust from the rear wheels, taking off fast so that, even if it only lasted a couple of seconds, he could say it had happened: a coyote joyriding in the back of his truck. Oh, this was one for the books! The stuff of legends! Word would get around, and from now on at the Sixshooter, they'd be saying, "Hey, Ray, what kind of perfume you using on your traps that you got 'em chasing after you?" and "Hey, Ray, pick up any more of those hitchhiker coyotes lately?" Oh yeah, this was grand, really something!

Claws scrabbling, Dinty Moore fought his way forward and turned around in time to see Brand X, standing stock-still in a rut of the jeep trail, already looking forlornly distant in the thick dust.

Draper slapped the steering wheel exultantly every time he checked the rearview mirror to make sure he still had a real live coyote riding back there like a family dog. Sometimes he swung his whole torso around to look through the rear window at it, just to see it with his own eyes instead of in the mirror, and, yup, sure enough, there it was: a coyote, standing back there with its legs all splayed out, the wind pinning back its ears, and its tongue hanging sideways out of its mouth.

Draper suddenly had a troubling thought. What if no one believed him? Although not exactly a bald-faced liar, he had been known to fancy up the truth. He needed witnesses. If that loose coyote would just stay put until he hit blacktop, then he could go so fast it'd know better than to bail out, and he could go driving past the 7-11 or the Frostee Freeze or the liquor store where there was bound to be someone in the parking lot who knew him.

No, better yet, the Gulf! *El Golfo!* That was it! If that coyote stayed in the truck until he hit blacktop, he'd shoot right down Highway 95 to Somerton—he was already south of Yuma—and on down to San Luis, a border town whose main business on the U.S. side was selling Mexican car insurance to American tourists, and then just an hour more to the fishing village of Santa Clara where he would pay Constanza a friendly little visit.

Draper got so distracted thinking about Constanza that a few minutes went by without his checking on Dinty Moore. When, with a start, he did remember to look, he didn't see him. Twisting around to look out the rear window, he jerked the steering wheel, and the truck yawed in and out of the ruts. Before he turned back, he caught a glimpse of Dinty Moore, and his shoulders sagged with relief. He hadn't seen him at first because he had moved up closer to the cab and was nosing and pawing at the gunnysack with the chloroformed bitch in it.

As the chloroform wore off, Chieko moaned and her legs thrust against the gunnysack. When she was woozily conscious enough to know that she did not know where she was but that she was imprisoned, the gunnysack bulged and wrinkled as she struggled in alarm. Dinty Moore lay down against it so that she could know he was there with her—and, also, in hope that his scent would be the first to reach her, rather than that of her sister's gunnysacked carcass, lying against the hump of the wheel well.

At last Chieko became still, and he felt her nose push out against the burlap and into his fur, and, when she identified him, her tail wagged feebly, moving the burlap slightly up and down; then her muzzle turned away from him, and he could hear her nose sniffing to find out if Brand X was there, too. Dinty Moore felt apologetic that it was only himself.

She smelled rotting flesh, and, because she did not know how long it had been since she had been forced to breathe the smell that had made the world turn purple then black and cave in on her, she did not know it could not be Brand X she was smelling. Her head jerked up in the gunnysack as she tried to penetrate the overpowering stench to know whose flesh it was.

When she suddenly realized it was her sister, the bulge of Chieko's raised head sank within the gunnysack, and she lay still for a long time, weak with gladness that it was not Brand X but jolted it was her sister. Their blood-tie asserted itself, and she did not rejoice as she had thought she would that her sister's path had ended.

She tried to backtrack through events to understand how her sister, whom she had last seen following Kodak, could now be where she was. The throb of her swollen leg brought back to her having tried to free herself from the trap by gnawing it off, but there hadn't been time; the two-legged had come right away. She began to understand that he had come too soon for her and too late for her sister. But, nauseous from the chloroform and its lingering, clinging smell, heartsick for Brand X, and jarred by her sister's death, she was too confused to pursue questions. All she knew was that her sister's path had ended and Brand X was not there and she was in a woven, inescapable, tight world.

The truck turned, bounced hard twice, then the wind swept through the gunnysack much faster, and there was a new smoothness. Dinty Moore stood up and looked out the lowered tailgate and saw a paved, black road unrolling beneath the truck.

"Home free!" Draper said.

Twenty minutes later, he roared into the border town of San Luis. He eased into a lane leading to the fluorescent-lit U.S. Border Inspection booths. Although he knew the border police were much more scrupulous about who and what came into the U.S. than who and what went out of it, the border routine always made him jumpy even when he had nothing to be jumpy about; but now, with a dead, stinking coyote in one gunnysack, a chloroformed bitch in another, and a loose one pacing around the bed of his pickup, he had so much to be jumpy about he was afraid to even light up a cigarette for fear it would be a dead giveaway he was jumpy about something.

"Whatcha got there?" the Border Inspection officer said in a voice trained to sound inquisitive in a friendly rather than overbearing way.

"Pooch for my gal down in Santa Clara," Draper said. "Watch out though. He ain't none too friendly with strangers."

"Yeah, so I see," he said, eyeing Dinty Moore cringed back against the hump of the wheel well with his hackles standing up like porcupine quills and his lip twitching in a terrified snarl. "Got a rabies certificate for it? You can't bring it back into the States without one."

"Like I said, he'll be staying down in Santa Clara."

"What kind is it anyway? Looks just like a coyote."

"Pedigreed mutt, but, yeah, there's probably some coyote kickin' around in him somewheres."

"How long will you be staying in Mexico?" he said, resuming his tone of official inquiry.

"Overnight oughta do it," Draper said, winking.

The officer stepped back from the cab of the pickup, glanced distastefully at the coyote and all the clutter in the bed of the pickup, then made a choppy, go-ahead hand signal.

Draper let out the clutch and glanced in the rearview mirror. He saw Dinty Moore hunker down beside the gunnysack containing Chieko.

"Good doggie, what a nice doggie," he sneered.

As he passed the bi-lingual Welcome to Mexico sign, Draper popped the tab on his last beer, lit up his next to last cigarette, slapped the steering wheel, and said, "Turn back the covers, Constanza! I'm comin'!"

21

Freedom cannot be granted. It must be taken.

MAX STIRNER, *The Ego and His Own*

It was seventy-four miles on high-banked, two-lane blacktop from the Mexican border to the Gulf, and there were only two villages in between. Riito was so small its train station had no clock, and El Doctor was a crossroads with a one-pump gas station and outhouse on one corner and two dilapidated general stores on diagonal corners. At Riito, Draper didn't even lift his foot off the gas pedal. Before banging over the railroad crossing, he just glanced down the tracks of the Ferrocarril Sonora & Baja California to be sure nothing was coming.

Dinty Moore had become so single-minded in his effort to free Chieko from the gunnysack that, until the truck bounced hard over the railroad crossing, he had even forgotten he was in it. By and large, he concentrated his efforts on the knot, but sometimes, in frustration, he seized a wad of the stubborn, brown burlap and shook it furiously, oblivious to how jarring it was to Chieko within. She tried to keep herself curled small to allow his teeth more of the gunnysack and to protect herself from them. The bunched fibers of the bulky knot were at least something he could grab hold of and get his teeth into. Unaware that his saliva had further tightened the knot, he yanked and tugged and gnawed at it. He braced his forelegs against Chieko's body and pulled back on it. He held the knot down with a paw while he worried it. Finally, by accident, he hooked a fang through it, and, in jerking his head to free it, the frayed knot came undone.

Chieko's head sprang out as if a compressing weight had been lifted from it. She touched Dinty Moore's muzzle with her nose. The gunnysack collapsed in rumpled folds behind her as she crawled out of it. She gazed around wildly and, in the reddish glow from the taillights, saw the bulging gunnysack that contained her sister's carcass. She cringed away, her back hunched and her tail pulled between her legs.

Looking out the back of the truck, she saw an unknown, night-shaped world streaming away from her at a queasily mesmerizing speed. Buffeted by the ear-pinning wind of its speed, she fought the truck bed's slick metal grooves for a foothold. When she tipped her muzzle to try to get her bearings by scent, air rushed up her nostrils so fast she could not breathe. Having believed that to be free of the gunnysack would be full-fledged freedom, she now saw that she was still held captive.

But Dinty Moore, now that he had accomplished her release from the gunnysack, knew only that he had done the thing he had had to do to enable them both to jump free. He crawled out onto the lowered tailgate and glanced back at Chieko to come, but she was hunched up with her head turned and didn't see him signal her.

He looked over the edge of the tailgate, straight down at the blurry blackness spinning from beneath the truck, and saw that the pavement where he and Chieko would land was moving too fast to jump down onto it; it would yank their legs out from under them and tumble them like sticks in a flash flood. His hopes of escape dashed, he crawled back from the brink, and the only thing he was glad of was that Chieko had not seen him beckon her out onto the lowered tailgate.

"Well goddammit!" Draper said, checking the rearview mirror and seeing Chieko crouched down by the jerry can. "I know I knotted that bag up good."

In his anger, he lit a cigarette before remembering it was his last one, the one he had been saving up for his triumphant arrival in El Golfo de Santa Clara. He'd had it all planned out—how he'd come barrelling into town, slewing around on those sand traps they called streets down there; radio blasting, hazard lights flashing, he'd swing by the *Delagación de Policía* and the open-air stalls of stolen goods and cheap junk set up under strings of colored lights down by the beachfront dance pavilion; laying on the horn, he'd slam to a stop out front of Constanza's shack, the whole family piling out onto the rickety porch in time to see a real live coyote riding in the bed of the pickup before it bailed out and took off.

But now that the chloroformed bitch had come to and somehow or other gotten herself out of the gunnysack, the two of them would be long gone the first time he slowed down. He knew right where it would be, too—the tight right-hand curve just before the road dropped off the mesa and went down between the cliffs—and knew his only hope of having two joyriding, genuine coyotes to show off in Santa Clara was to have a lead foot going through that curve. The beers he had drunk gave him the Dutch courage to think he could do it.

It was a notoriously dangerous curve. A sign depicted its curvature with a thick, triple-shafted arrow ending at a single arrow head; a series of signs counted down in meters the narrowing distance to it and gave dual warnings to reduce speed to forty kilometers/twenty-five miles-per-hour; and a final, bi-lingual, red-and-white-stripe-bordered sign of billboard size screamed in enormous, red letters: ¡PELIGRO! DANGER! A long, single row of short, white crosses lined the approach to the curve: one for each victim the curve had claimed. There were so many it looked like a miniature white picket fence. The wooden crosses were mounted on little white plaster domes with the name of the victim and the date of the fatality painted in black. Propped against many of the domes were bouquets of sun-faded, plastic flowers, and hanging from the crossbars were gold or silver chains with crosses and Saint Christopher medals.

Out in the dirt, between the second and third warning signs, was a vast pile of wreckage: the recovered vehicles that had missed the curve and gone over the cliff. The crosses were for the memory of the dead; but the sky-high pile of twisted, shattered, crushed vehicles was intended as an object lesson for the living.

Draper had always liked the curve. It broke up the monotony of the drive, and it signalled the home stretch. After the road curved hard to the right to shoot down a cleft in the high mud cliffs, it was only nine miles to Santa Clara. That last stretch paralleled the Gulf, but sand dunes blocked it from view.

Now, though, with the pressure on, Draper entered the curve too fast and, realizing it too late, tried to scrub off speed in the middle of it. He was tapping the brake pedal when he hit a fresh patch of oil. The truck slewed. The tires squealed. The headlights swung around like searchlights. The outside rear wheel hit some gravel on the edge of the road, and the truck slid out still closer to the plummeting drop-off just beyond the narrow strip of gravel at the lip. The truck was moving more sideways than forward, and there was a suspended moment when it had slowed to a near standstill.

The gunnysack with Salem in it careened to the other side of the truck bed and thumped against the hump of the wheel well. Chieko, with her legs splayed out, fought the truck's leaning to get away from it. Dinty Moore was thrown hard against her. They felt the speed slacken and the moment come when the truck was suspended between plunging over the edge or squeaking through the curve's apex.

Their eyes locked and said *now*. They scrabbled out onto the lowered tailgate and, hunching up their backs, pounced onto the gravel-strewn black pavement as if it were prey they were starved for. They bounded away across the mesa, tails streaming, eyes glowing, giddy with liberty, rejoicing at once again being in sole command of themselves—of their own direction, their own leg-speed. Freedom made the pain of her hurt leg trivial. They paused to pass water, then ran to the edge of the high, mud cliffs.

Below them, they saw the truck reach the bottom of the steep road that went down between the cliffs. It had grown so small with distance that it was hard for them to imagine that only a minute before they had been captive in it.

As they stood at the edge of the faceted, jutting cliffs, they caught a distant, rhythmic sound. Exchanging a questioning glance, Chieko and Dinty Moore closed their jaws to silence their panting. With pricked ears, testing noses, and puzzled eyes, they scanned the air and land to find out what the sound came from.

After a broad band of flat, bare land lying between the base of the cliffs and the road came a phalanx of sand dunes. The sight of the towering, white dunes filled Chieko with such leaden dread of having to cross them that she started to turn her head away. But her eye was caught by a vast, dark, sparkling plain beyond the dunes, and the rhythmic, soothing sound seemed to be coming from it. It was the blackest, flattest, most utterly barren land she had ever seen, and the only land she had ever heard that sounded as if it were breathing. Then, with a shock, Chieko realized that what she was seeing and hearing was not land at all.

22

It is a great journey to the world's end.

ENGLISH PROVERB

Stupefied with rapture, Chieko and Dinty Moore stood at the brink of the high mud cliffs and saw it spread out before them in all its stupendous vastness: Skywater. Their unslakable eyes drank in the sight of water as far and wide as they could see. Again and again, they traced its immensity, from its beginning at the white-ruffled shoreline, then out to the moving, molten masses of it, then out farther to the glassy, smooth flat of it, then out and out still farther to where it touched the entire length of the sky.

Chieko stayed within her silence; but Dinty Moore could not stop his throat from whining with joy. With Skywater spread out before them, the allegiance of their spirits to it rose up strongly within them. Indeed, looking out over Skywater, Chieko had the sensation that her spirit had leaped from her, leaving her behind on the cliff's edge as it surged forward to end its exile from its homeland.

For a short while, the clamor of astonishment and the revelry of joy within them drowned out Brand X's absence.

But, as their joy quieted, their thoughts turned to him, and, having been standing shoulder to shoulder, Chieko and Dinty Moore moved apart to make a place where Brand X belonged. She turned her head to look over her shoulder at the dark masses of the land behind her. A moan climbed her throat at how much of it there was. The truck's speed had obliterated her ability to gauge how far she had travelled, but she knew, however far it was, that it was one thing to be carried on a black trail like a stick made swift by rushing water and quite another for Brand X, with only his own legs—and one of them all but useless—to cover the same distance.

As she turned away in despair from her survey of the endless land behind her, she caught a glimpse, off in the distance to the west, of what appeared to be a river.

Like the coyotes who had set out on the journey—Brand X, Dinty Moore, Chieko, Salem, Kodak, Kraft, and Boyardee, the waters of the Colorado River that reached the sea were greatly diminished. The sun was only a petty thief of the river's waters; it was humans who had purloined it, deviating it into irrigation canals and laking it behind dams. The stingy allotment of water permitted to reach land's end ignored the urgent, ancient, laudable desire of the river to surge full-strength to the sea. Its once mighty, rampaging mouth was now a sprawling delta of mud flats and lazy channels sluggishly draining its meager remnants into the sea.

But, seeing a flowing water-trail that had made it through the desert and into Skywater, Chieko's eyes babbled wild hopes and burned with a wish so intense that it almost seemed accomplished fact: if only Brand X could find this broad water-trail, it would lead him not only to Skywater but also to her.

She spun around joyfully and nipped Dinty Moore's neck. Dinty Moore mistook her high spirits for journey-pride at having reached Skywater, and he wholeheartedly joined in her playful mood. They chased each other along the cliff tops, pivoting, rearing up to bat at each other, dropping down onto their forelegs with their hindquarters in the air, then leaping up and tearing off again.

When at last they stood with lolling tongues and heaving sides, Chieko avoided Dinty Moore's eyes out of embarrassment at her unwonted friskiness; but he nudged her shoulder and, when she turned her head, caught her eye to issue her a grinning challenge to race him to Skywater.

They plunged down the face of the mud-faceted, pyramidal cliff and tore across the short, flat stretch of ground between the base of the cliffs and the high dunes now hiding the water from view. Being younger by far, she was well in the lead despite her injured leg. Without pausing to work up the courage to cross it, she dashed across the road that led to Santa Clara and began to lunge up the sloping, white wall of sand that was all that stood between her and Skywater.

As she clambered up the fine, white sand of the dune, it struck her that this dune seemed no different than all the other dunes she and Brand X and Dinty Moore had slogged their way up and down when there had been no prospect of Skywater lying just over the summit, and the appalling thought came to her: what if it is not there now either?

But when she crested the dune, it was there; and its sudden, sparkling blue-black aliveness and thereness made her rear back on her haunches, her tail uncertain whether to curl under in submission to it or greet it with joyful wagging.

A smooth beach spread out from the base of the dunes like a bravado cape, tantalizing, taunting the surf to charge upon it, to trample it. But the low-tide waves coming and going from the sandy beach were gentle, lethargic, barely energetic enough to curl over on themselves and make a ragged ruffle of foam.

The surf's gentle sound lulled her with its eloquence, filled her with an easeful, oblivious peace, as if she were lying curled in milk-fed drowsiness against her mother's body, hearing her mother's muffled heartbeat, the voice of her mother's heart like the voice of Skywater—soothing, rhythmic, mysterious.

It had never occurred to her that Skywater would have a voice of its own. Although most of the water she had known was mute—the water in the metal tank and in stagnant water holes—she had heard the roar of thick, roiling water slamming down water-trails, the trickle and patter and plink of rain, and the strident splurge of ephemeral waterfalls hurling themselves over sheer canyon walls. But the voice she heard now she recognized as being the true voice of water, free of land and obedient to no laws except its own.

Dinty Moore's raspy pant as he fought his way up the dune intruded on her moment. Overwhelmed by Skywater, she had entirely forgotten him; but, having gotten there first, she now felt a proprietary pride in what he was about to behold, as if it were hers to offer him.

He stopped and looked up at the statue of her standing atop the dune, ignoring him, transfixed by whatever she was seeing but that he could not yet see. And since she had not rushed to drink, he faltered over the reluctant thought that the seeming water he had seen from the cliffs had been a false water-place, a mirage. He scrambled grimly the rest of the way up the dune to get the catastrophic disillusionment he believed was in store for him over with quickly.

He clambered to the top of the dune, saw what Chieko was seeing, and gave a yip of joy; then, in the same spirit in which flags are planted and markers imbedded to commemorate historic arrivals, he sniffed carefully for a worthy spot, cocked his leg against the dried stalk of a sand verbena, and passed a long stream of water in proclamation that he, Dinty Moore, a moon-caller from far, far away, had stood there.

Chieko did the same. Her intention, however, was not to make an announcement at large but rather to convey a private message to Brand X that she was there awaiting him.

With an exchange of glances, they plunged eagerly down the Skywater side of the dune, came to a ten-foot dropoff where sand overlaid the top of a short, mud bluff, its exposed face a replica in miniature of the high cliffs, and leaped off its edge. They landed in dry sand above the high-tide line where brown, viny strands of small-bulbed, rubbery kelp lay abandoned by the water. They raced across the beach, noticing how much faster they ran as the sand grew firmer with dampness, and came to the darker wetness of the sand only recently exposed by the retreating tide.

They ran into the water to the tops of their forelegs, and the shock of being in it, of standing in Skywater, made both of them forget they had raced to see who would be first and made Chieko oblivious to the water's sting on her wounded leg. Standing in Skywater, smelling its scent and surrounded by its voice, they were stunned to find themselves perched on the very brink of arrival at Brand X's destination. Only when the water of Skywater was on their tongues would it truly have been reached. They had entered the water just after a wave had broken and were standing in its foamy backwash. Now the water pulled back from them, and suddenly they were left barelegged, empty-mouthed.

Standing atop the dune, Chieko had watched the waves come in and go out, and so she knew the water would soon return to them. But no water Dinty Moore had ever seen came *back*. Water in a wash always moved in only one direction and, once gone, never turned around and came back again. Too impatient to wait, he chased after the receding water, so that the new, incoming wave lifted him off his feet and carried him with it to shore, depositing him like a wayward pup.

As the next wave came toward them, swirling around their legs and tugging at the rocky sand beneath their paws, they lowered their muzzles and lapped furiously at it. When the wave receded from them, they stood with dripping muzzles and did not look at each other. The next wave came, and again they drank. Avoiding each other's eyes, they moved apart to drink from other places.

When a new wave came to their new places, they lowered their heads with their original eagerness and lapped at it. Still not daring to hazard a glance at each other for fear of seeing confirmation of their dreadful suspicion, they trotted still farther apart and stood waiting for the water to come to them.

Chieko was the first to give up. She stopped changing positions, now here, now there, farther out, closer in, trying to find the right spot to drink from, and simply stood staring out at the faraway forever of Skywater, ignoring the water that came and went around her legs. The certainty that the journey had been in vain glazed her eyes: Skywater was undrinkable.

Dinty Moore, refusing to believe it, raced frantically back and forth along the shoreline, dipping his head to lap tentatively, warily, as if he knew better but could not stop himself. At last, he too gave up, letting the water dribble back out of his mouth. Then, his sides heaving, head hung between his bony shoulder blades, he retched.

Of all the places that Dinty Moore had drunk from in his life—scummed, stagnant waterholes; coyote wells dug in dry washes; the two-leggeds' water tank; an arroyo's rusty porridge; a river; stones with drops of condensation cupped in a hollow; irrigation canals—never before in his life had he drunk from a place whose water made him thirsty. Water was meant to get rid of thirst. That was what water was for. The merciless proof that Skywater was not meant to be drunk lay simply in its having increased rather than eased his thirst.

Chieko turned her head toward shore, and Dinty Moore gave her a long, hard look, then his eyes changed, and he threw back his head and yipped. Chieko watched him carefully as he pawed and snapped at the foam, water drooling from his lips as he yipped in a not-right way that chilled her blood. Throwing his muzzle skyward, he yipped with dreadful hilarity to the moon, as if he and the moon were sharing an uproarious private joke.

Skywater's brine, Dinty Moore had decided, was the final, cruel jest on all thirsty beings from the sun-dazed lands. Spite water! Skywater was spite water, Dinty Moore yipped to the moon.

Chieko threw him a stern glance over her shoulder and was relieved to see his eyes register the reprimand and waver, and, although he continued to yip, his yipping now had a forced, begrudging note. She turned her head away from him and, leaving the water, went and sat on the firm, damp sand just beyond the reach of the waves. The dark, wet sand looked like a shadow cast by the water onto the land, a shadow memory of when its reach had been high upon the land. Looking out at Skywater, she listened to Dinty Moore's broken-spirited laughter dwindle into sporadic yips then subside altogether.

He plodded out of the shallow shoreline water and came and lay down close to where she was sitting. He laid his chin on the damp sand between his forelegs, and the bumps of his raised eyebrows, with the whiskers on them moving like antennae, added to the disconsolate, chastened look of his eyes. She did not know what conclusion he had come to, but whatever it was, he had returned to his senses and now knew that it was no laughing matter that the journey, with all of its terrible consequences, had all been for nothing.

After a little while, looking out at the vast, sparkling, stupendous immensity of Skywater's undrinkable, sacred water, a quiet understanding came over her that Skywater was spirit water, water intended only for the spirits of the dead. She and Dinty Moore had reached a place they were not intended to have reached. They did not belong here. They were intruders, trespassers at the water-place of spirits. That was why they could not drink from Skywater. It was not meant for them; they were living beings. Only the spirits of desert beings were meant to quench their thirst in Skywater.

She looked gravely out at the glittering water, and all at once Skywater seemed laden with the invisible, buoyant spirits of all the moon-callers whose paths, whether completed or not, had ended. Skywater was *their* water-place. Then the inevitable, devastating thought came to her that perhaps it was Brand X's, too.

She began to pace along the shoreline's sinuous edge, her head turned to look at its undulating, moon-shimmered surface. Every so often, she stopped, faced the water and, with her eyes squeezed shut, cried out to the spirit-bearing water in a voice so bereft, so forsaken that, finally, Dinty Moore got up and followed her, trotting along just behind her, stopping when she stopped, joining his voice with hers, keeping her company on her solitary vigil for the spirit of Brand X.

23

Alone, alone, all all alone,
Alone on a wide wide sea!
And never a saint took pity on
My soul in agony.

S. T. COLERIDGE,
The Rime of the Ancient Mariner

At the spot where Brand X entered Mexico, there was no fence to belly under, no bi-lingual sign, no visible line of demarcation. The Sonoran desert, all of a piece, looked the same on one side of the border as on the other.

In the course of the night, Brand X had gained finesse at favoring his gunshot shoulder while still making good progress. He had worked out a rhythm of trotting along on three legs and using the fourth only to lightly tap the ground. The punctuation of the tap somehow served to coordinate his stride. He looked like something which, although broken, works well in a makeshift way. He could not remember what it had been like to use all four legs.

Throughout the night, coyotes had called out to him to identify himself, but he had not answered them. The only coyotes he had acknowledged were illusory; his mind kept playing a cruel trick on him, making him forget that Dinty Moore and Chieko were gone. Time and again, trotting along, he had turned his head toward one or the other of them and had been shocked blank at finding their customary places at his flanks empty. Remembering why, he suffered the loss of them all over again. Each time it happened he was pierced by such loneliness for them that he felt as if he had swallowed a sharp rock.

He longed for Chieko, for the tilt of her head when attending to a sound and the companionship of her black-rimmed, golden brown eyes. He missed Dinty Moore's long grin of muzzle and was heartstruck every time he thought of what courageous loyalty it had taken for Dinty Moore to have jumped into the truck on his behalf. Brand X's adamant intention at the outset of his journey was now like a prophecy bitterly fulfilled; he was indeed going to Skywater alone, on his own, leader of none, companion of none, place-sharer of none.

Since the sun would soon be climbing the sky, Brand X concentrated on hunting food. He caught two lizards whose night-cooled blood had made them sluggish and snatched a ground squirrel before it could dash into its hole. Although the dunes and the sun-baked, cracked-mud mosaic of the Yuma Desert's dry lake beds lay behind him, his choices of shelter were still sparse. He nosed and scraped at the pinkish brown ground under a creosote bush then flopped down and, heaving a sigh, laid his muzzle on his forepaws.

Facing south, he studied the terrain he would be crossing that night, looking for signs of dry water-trails. His eyes grew heavy and were almost closed when he noticed something white, like a small piece of cloud, drifting low across the sky. His eyes snapped open, and he was about to call it to the attention of Dinty Moore and Chieko when he remembered in time.

It flew directly overhead, and Brand X could see astonishingly long, black legs trailing the length of its body. It was a heron, a vagrant great egret that had wandered from the irrigation canals that watered the Mexican farmlands south of San Luis. Its arched wings were long and broad; its beak long and yellow. An extravagance of feathers swept off its back into a train. But it was the pure whiteness of its plumage that captivated Brand X.

This cloud bird looked as if it knew of things he knew nothing about. He wanted to call out to it, to question it. Where was it from? Was the sky its burrow and air its food? Did it have a place-sharer? Perhaps, he suddenly thought, this was the spirit of a bird and this spirit bird had flown here from Skywater. Or perhaps this was what the spirits of *all* Skywater beings looked like.

Then another thought struck him, one so alarming it made him scramble to his feet, made his heart crowd his ribs, his hackles stand up along the ridge of his back, and his throat feel as if a wad of gristle were lodged in it. Perhaps Chieko's path had ended in the gunnysack, and this was *her* spirit, fresh from Skywater, flying above him to let him know—and to lead him there.

Brand X scanned the blue sky with his golden eyes, scouring the skies for another spirit bird. If this was Chieko, then Dinty Moore must be close by. He would not have let her go to Skywater alone; he would have accompanied her there, and he would be with her now.

In the last part of the sky where he looked, with the back of his head pushed hard against his neck, what he saw instead of a second, dreaded, white-feathered spirit was his father's white eye, paled by daylight. It should have long since been in its den beneath the mountains, but there it was, an unobtrusive intruder, an outsider in the sun's domain. Although accustomed to the thick pile of night, it was somehow managing to cling to the smooth glaze, the slippery blue of day. Insubstantial, frail, sun-blinded, it was a ghost of itself; yet it was there.

Brand X watched the lone bird as it flew across his father's eye: white lost on white, melding, then separating, each again discrete—one round, the other elegantly elongated. He watched the heron flying south until it became an aerial fleck he wasn't quite certain he was still seeing.

He looked back up at his father's pale, persevering eye, then he closed his own eyes and, like one overwhelmed by an enchantment, went to sleep in the mottled shade of the creosote bush, under the aegis of his father's steadfast eye. He whimpered in his sleep, and his legs jerked. His eyelids flickered open, and his eyes, having rolled up into his head, were momentarily his father's, white and sightless.

24

I am always longing to be with men more excellent than myself.

CHARLES LAMB, letter to S. T. Coleridge

Parched from Skywater's saltwater, Chieko and Dinty Moore trotted to the delta of the Colorado River where they lapped brackish water from one of its sandbarred mouths. As he drank, Dinty Moore kept raising his head to look westward. At last, he stopped drinking and simply stood, ears forward, staring intently at a small island out in the moon-splashed sea.

Chieko glanced over at him and, noticing the rigid, riveted intensity of his body and gaze, looked to see what he was looking at. She saw a small, dark land shape floating far out on the water. She lifted her nose and tested the air, but the island was too far away to send any scents. Puzzled by his interest, she turned back to him and watched his tail begin to gently wag and a grin pull back his lips then split open his jaws—his old grin, not the sun-dazed one.

Her eyes ablaze with joyful surmise, Chieko yipped and, reaching out a forepaw, swiped at Dinty Moore's shoulder with eagerness to know what evidence of Brand X's presence he had.

Dinty Moore's head jerked toward her, and, seeing her eyes lit up with hope, he knew that she had misconstrued the grin brought forth by a sudden, stunning thought: the small hump of land out where water and sky were one might well be the home ground of the moon-caller who had bequeathed to all moon-callers his songs and desert wisdom. Seeing that he had inadvertently caused her to rejoice at the prospect of reunion with Brand X, his long grin vanished, and his tail sagged in apology.

Frantic for assurance, she swiped at him again. He pivoted away from her, then swung back to face her, his eyes remorseful for having misled her. He watched hope go out of her tail, her body, and, last of all, her face. Her quenched eyes had the confused, questioning look of one who has been badly mistreated for no reason whatsoever.

A stiffly formal silence engulfed them. Not knowing how to proceed with each other, how to end the awkwardness, they stood with hanging heads and lowered eyes and tails. Chieko finally decided that the only way to resume was to return to the starting point of the misunderstanding and go on from there as if it had not happened. Although she was no longer thirsty, she drank from the river, and Dinty Moore moved alongside her and, although not thirsty either, also drank.

There was no decision Dinty Moore had to make about what he was going to do. He knew he was going to swim to the hump of land surrounded by Skywater. Swimming was not the obstacle to his new journey; having swum across the Gila River, he now knew that his legs carried in them ancient memories of the time when water had covered the land and that they still remembered how to move through water. Chieko was his journey's obstacle. Loyalty to Brand X required him to stay with her. Since he could not leave her behind, he must convince her to come with him.

Dinty Moore trotted down a sandbar in the wide, flowing water-trail and waded out into Skywater. He turned his head toward her then pointed it at the island. She lay down on the sand to show him she did not accept his invitation to come. She did not know what it was about the island that had merited his grin, but, since it was not Brand X, she did not care. All she knew was that she was going to wait for Brand X at the place where the flowing water-trail joined Skywater.

To entice her, Dinty Moore waded out still farther and, again, turned his head toward her. Her tail thumped the ground in polite apology, but she did not budge.

Throwing a wistful look at the island, Dinty Moore waded out of the sea and began to restlessly pace along the shore as if saddled with a problem undeservedly foisted off on him. The more he paced the more her refusal to accompany him chafed him. After all, hadn't he accompanied *her*—jumped into a truck and freed her from the gunnysack? Wasn't it her turn now to go with him, however reluctantly?

As Chieko watched his impatient pacing, she felt his criticism of her in it and tried to understand why Dinty Moore so urgently wanted to go to the little chunk of land floating on Skywater. Since she knew it had been Dinty Moore's esteem for Brand X that had compelled him to make the journey to Skywater, Chieko sensed that he had given up on ever seeing Brand X again and now something else had made him willing to risk another long journey. A cold gust of sorrow spiralled through her.

Finally, Dinty Moore gave up on persuading her by his impatient pacing and brusquely trotted over to where she lay. He was reaching out his muzzle to bid her farewell when he glimpsed something moving out in the water, and his head twitched away from his intended farewell. Seeing his head jerk away from her, she looked to see what had caused it.

The fishing fleet from Santa Clara had set sail before

dawn. On the boats fanned out across the water not far off-shore, stick-figure two-leggeds could be seen lowering nets into the water. Chieko's heart was suffocated by an avalanche of despair. On land two-leggeds had hidden steel jaws to seize her leg in a bite from which there was no escape, and they had run down the little one as he tried to dash across their broad black trail, and they had swooped down from the sky to blast a ragged, bleeding hole into Brand X's body. And now, here they were in the haven of Skywater itself, setting about to capture and kill spirits.

Seeing them, she felt a great urgency for Dinty Moore to be gone before the boats came any closer. Scrambling to her feet, she brought her nose close to his, so close to touching that it felt like touch itself. He slid his muzzle along hers and gently took hold of the white patch of her cheek fur and shook it gently. Wanting him to hurry, she pulled her head out of his grasp and, with an upsurge of affection, gave him a quick nudge toward the water. He glanced at her with surprise, and she saw his remorse at leaving her dissolve into gratitude for her encouraging his departure.

He ran into the foamy surf and, tipping up his muzzle, breasted the crest of an incoming wave. The deepening water lifted him off his feet and covered his body. His head, as if decapitated by the sea, moved slowly out into Skywater.

Chieko watched him until the tips of his tall, pointed ears were too small to see. As she watched, she sensed that as Brand X had set forth for Skywater to heed an ancient yearning for the time when water had been bountiful and thirst unknown, so too was Dinty Moore, in striking out for the island in Skywater, answering a summons carried in his blood.

The sun rose, and the sea, faithfully imitating the sky, turned blue. Chieko stayed on the beach, with her ears pointed forward and her squinting eyes fixed on the island out in the glittering blue. As the sun climbed high overhead, she moved back near the base of a sand dune to crouch in the spindly, spidery shade of a clump of white bursage.

When she thought he had had time to reach the floating land, she returned to the shore and called out to him, raising her throat to the sky and shutting her eyes tight; but, though she listened hard, she heard no reply. She reminded herself that it was a very long way for even a moon-caller's voice to carry, and she tried not to think what a long way, too, it was for a moon-caller's legs to swim.

 **25**

Albert,

It sure seems queer to be writing you a letter when you're sitting right over there on the breezeway in plain sight. But you know how I never could bring myself to apologize out loud to you. So, same as ever, I'm putting it in writing instead, just like when we'd squabble as kids, and I'd go drop a little bitty folded up scrap of paper with an IOU for 1 apology in your mailbox and ring the doorbell and go scooting back home.

I must be pretty set in my ways, writing this letter for you to find like an IOU after I have passed on, all because I can't bring myself to say to your dear old sweet face how sorry I am to be leaving you behind. I know I can't hold on much longer though, and I just want to tell you I am dreadful sorry for it.

I truly think I'd of lasted a lot longer if it wasn't for those tailings from the old copper mines. I don't mean to say our water getting poisoned did it. I mean us being put to the bother and the lifting and the expense of that bottled water, and, worst yet, the critters no longer coming around to drink from our tank and keep us company.

I swear to goodness I wish we had never seen it in the paper about those tailings the same as I wish I had never seen that picture of poor old Kraft! Then we could of just gone on the same as usual. Old as we are, it would have been a toss-up whether it was the water or our age that killed us, and, as for the critters, their lives are short enough the water most likely wouldn't have had time to do them harm either.

Now don't overly trouble yourself about what to do with my remains. There's plenty enough wood in the scrap pile for you to bang together a box. Just don't you go carting me off to some funeral parlor in Yuma! I don't want any strangers fiddling with me. It doesn't matter one bit to me what I am buried in. A nightgown, clean socks, and my usual tramping-around shoes would suit me fine.

Even after all these years I still can't find words for my sorrow over losing our Pete. We had a fine boy.

Well, I've got just this one last thing to say to you, Albert Ryder. I thank you for the life you have given me by pulling up stakes thirty-nine years ago and bringing us out here to the Kofas. I have lived like royalty.

Your Hallie Durham Ryder

P.S. Whatever you do, don't you dare bury me in that sad old polka-dotted dress!

26

Journeys end in lovers meeting.

WILLIAM SHAKESPEARE, *Twelfth Night*

The delta of the river flanged and forked into several streams. Brand X was studying them to decide which one to follow when, with shocking abruptness, he saw that it did not matter. The vast blackness in the distance which he had taken to be a flat of extraordinary barrenness was Skywater itself.

Exultant with arrival, he stared at it so hard that his eyes felt dry. Joy burbled in his throat, and, feeling his spirit thrash within him like something trapped trying to get free, he discovered that the arduous accomplishment of his spirit's yearning gave rise in him, oddly enough, not so much to a sense of fulfillment as to a heightened understanding of the depth of the yearning itself.

Looking up at the curved, white claw of moon above the sea, he saw it, as he always had, as his father's white marble eye, and he regretted that tonight it was so heavy-lidded. A thin strand of disappointment crept through his elation that his father's eye, seeing him on the brink of his journey's destination, had not opened wide with pride of him.

He set off at his wounded trot across the hardened mud flats of the delta. At the place where the fork he was following flowed into Skywater, he saw a coyote shape rise from the sand. Hope flew up in him like a bevy of startled quail. He sternly reproved himself, telling himself that since he had not recognized Skywater for what it was, how dare he think he recognized that distant moon-caller? He further admonished his hope by remembering that Chieko would not be alone as that one out there was; Dinty Moore would be with her. Brand X tamped down his hopes, turning round and round on them with the firmness of paws smoothing the ground of a prospective shelter; but, undaunted as wildflowers, they sprang back up. The certainty that he was, at long last, approaching Skywater played havoc in him with the uncertain identity of the coyote standing on its shore.

Chieko did not know what made her fur prickle and her heart suddenly startle with a premonition of joy. Having waited out so many suns under skimpy bushes in the sand and watched the moon-eye close, night by night, until now it was nearly blind, she suddenly stood up as if she knew her vigil was over. Turning her head, she saw him and, at a distance defiant of all her senses, knew him with a completeness that seemed unconscious.

Seeing her know him, he immediately recognized her, and the absoluteness of his recognition turned his censured hope into unbridled jubilation.

Neither of them called out. Neither broke into headlong running. As if leery of shimmering water that might prove to be a mirage, they moved toward each other with such cautiously wagging, stiff-legged wariness that their ardor had the look of enmity.

Chieko whined softly as he came near. She noticed the makeshift gait he had perfected. He noticed her briny, new smell. Each noticed the stark gauntness of the other. They registered these changes, these not-likenesses, then put them aside in favor of all that was familiar.

She bowed her head as he came still nearer, not in coyness or submission but in a surfeit of emotion. Her body quivered and writhed with welcome. He touched her nose with his, then rubbed the length of his long, thin muzzle along hers. Turning his face into hers, he gently bit her cheeks, first one side, then, turning her head with his muzzle, the other side. He moved his muzzle along the length of her, burying his nose, burrowing into her fur, nibbling her. Standing side to side, head to tail, tails wagging, they rubbed their bodies, their entire body lengths, against each other.

She held still until she could hold still no longer, then she pawed the air and curved her head toward his head at her flank to look quickly but directly into his eyes. Their eyes had to veer away from their stunning glimpse into one another's spirit; the intensity of their happiness was so overwhelming that they had to hastily recoil from it to prevent their spirits from soaring away. Caught in the backwash of the immense moment, Chieko felt the need to anchor her spirit, and, floundering for something mundane to preoccupy her, fell to digging a gratuitous hole in the easy sand. Brand X, also at a loss in the wake of their penetrating glimpse, began to sniff the air and look around in an inquiring way, as if to locate something that should have been there but wasn't.

Chieko, raising her head from the hole, observed his inquiry and suddenly realized it was Dinty Moore he was searching for. She had been so overjoyed by Brand X's arrival that she had forgotten about Dinty Moore, but now all of the clamorous things which Brand X did not know about crowded into her mind: Dinty Moore's departure for the floating land; her sister's path having ended; Skywater being a water-place only for spirits. She began to dig more rapidly, as if to recover something crucial she had just remembered having buried there. Sand flew up between her hind legs, pelting Brand X.

He jumped aside and looked at her as if he were trying to figure out what had suddenly made her dig so frantically, why her tail now sagged with sadness and the sidelong looks she gave him when she raised her head from the hole seemed to beg him to stop peering around and testing the air.

He nudged her flank to get her attention. With her hind legs on the rim of the hole and her forelegs deep within it, she was so steeply slanted down into the hole that he could not see her head. At his nudge, she stopped digging and raised her head, her nose granular with sand, to look up at him from the bottom of the hole. He looked around and smelled the air insistently, then cocked his head, awaiting her reply.

She ducked her head back down into the hole and resumed her frantic digging. He nudged her again, harder this time. She backed out of the hole and, giving him a beckoning look, walked reluctantly to the water's edge and pointed her nose at the bump of land far out in Skywater.

Brand X looked where she was pointing, then jerked his head incredulously toward her. She glanced at him and pointed her nose adamantly at the island again.

Brand X walked with great formality into the lacy froth at Skywater's edge and on out through it until his legs were alternately submerged and bared by the coming and going of the waves. He stopped and turned to face the island crouched like a small, dark creature on the faintly moonlit surface of the water and, tilting his muzzle skyward, sent his voice arching like a rainbow of song up through the night air and down to the rainbow's end on the island. He did not know if he was singing to Dinty Moore on the island or to Dinty Moore's spirit in Skywater, but, whichever it was, he knew that he would never see him again.

As he sang his farewell, Brand X sorrowed for Dinty Moore, and his sorrow went into his song. Singing to him, he remembered Dinty Moore's long grin and the ancestral songs which no one could sing as he did and the brave loyalty of his accompanying Chieko in the truck. Brand X's heart bloomed with thankfulness to Dinty Moore for ignoring his rebuffs and having been a persistent companion and, by joining paths with him, making each of their paths wider. Although he thought Dinty Moore's path had ended, his heart nonetheless spoke the benediction universal among all living beings: May you live a completed path.

Ready now to drink from Skywater, Brand X lowered his muzzle to a fraction above the water swirling around his legs. He sniffed it perfunctorily in the disavowing way one smells something that is going to be consumed regardless of what its smell reveals; then he began to lap quickly at the water. The wrongness of its taste was immediately evident to him, but, because it was his journey's end to drink deeply from Skywater, he continued to drink in stubborn disbelief that the more of it he drank the thirstier he became. His tongue slowed and, eventually, he raised his head and looked at the water that had belied his ancestral faith in the one unfailing water-place.

But then, like Chieko and Dinty Moore before him, he hoped perhaps it was only the particular spot where he happened to be and not the whole of Skywater that was undrinkable, and he waded out farther in search of good water. He stopped in the shallow trough between the wave hitting shore and the breeze-wrinkled water piling up into the next wave. When the water there tasted exactly the same, he knew it was futile to keep trying elsewhere. Too leaden with despair to return to shore, he stayed where he was. When a wave moved past him it lifted him up and he had to hold his chin high, but the water gently set him back down again, and his paws touched bottom.

For quite some time, Brand X remained there, bobbing up and down. Now that he had discovered that Skywater incited instead of slaked the thirst of living beings, he well understood Dinty Moore's striking out for the island. Brand X wished that he too could find some use to make of Skywater, some other purpose it could serve him, since, as his burning thirst made clear, it did not serve the purpose water was meant to serve. He wished that, like Dinty Moore, he too could fabricate a new destination out of his devastating disillusionment with the one he had achieved.

At last, he drew his legs up under his body and let a wave deposit him on shore like flotsam. His soaked, briny fur clung to the ridged ripples of his ribs, and his tail, plastered to the tapering, trivial bone, dangled from him like a long crooked nail.

With the water slapping at his legs at the height of a sprung trap, he faced the molten, black immensity of the sea and, closing his eyes tightly, raised his long muzzle to his father's oblivious slit of eye, and hurled his voice up into the star-spattered sky. His howls spread up and outward until it seemed that a chorus of moon-caller voices drifted on the star trails.

Whining softly in her throat, Chieko crouched in the damp sand of the deep hole she had dug while his voice fell on her like a mountain.

When his parched voice finally broke off, Brand X opened his eyes and gazed around with a disoriented look, as if not only his voice but he himself had been flung out over Skywater. He shook himself, looked to see where Chieko was, and set off at a decisive trot along the erratic, jagged edge of the tideline.

At intervals paced off in his mind, he stopped and carefully sniffed the rim of thicker foam at a wave's leading edge and the skim of white bubbles swirling atop the wave when it climbed the shore. He had come to the conclusion that the foam and the bubbles were the saliva washed from the jaws of newly arrived, thirsty spirits when they bent their heads to take their first drink from Skywater, to drink the water only they could drink.

Each time he stopped, after sniffing the spirits' white-bubbled spittle, Brand X passed water. When the foamy, shallow water retreated from the shore, carrying his water in it, he moved on, satisfied that his scent was being borne out into Skywater to let the spirits of Dinty Moore, Kraft, Boyar-dee, and his brothers and sisters know that he, too, was there and greeted them from the shore.

Chieko watched anxiously as he moved farther and farther away from her along the shoreline, stopping to pass water then trotting on. He grew so small she feared he would disappear altogether, like Dinty Moore's tall ears in the water, never to return.

But he did return and, after exchanging greetings with her, went to the dry sand back toward the dunes and dug a narrow, sloping hole. Three feet down he came to damp sand and sat back to wait for the rainwater stored in the sand to seep into it. He drank the brackish water cupped in the hole until, hitting bottom, the underside of his tongue became gritty with sand. He waited for the well to refill itself and drank again.

His thirst modestly accommodated, he went back down to the damp sand and lay beside Chieko. Together they watched the sea change colors under the dawn sky until they were slit-eyed against the glittering immensities of a Skywater now sky-blue. He took delight in the way the sun danced on the water's skin, how it lit up at the sun's touch, and in the way the territories of sky and water shared a border at the horizon. Since the sun and the moon were place-sharers, surely Skywater was their offspring.

In its beauty Brand X found recompense for its water being useless to him. The amusing little spotted sandpipers skittering erratically along the shoreline diverted him from troubling thoughts of where to go now that he knew Skywater could not slake his thirst. He watched for the spirit bird he had seen in the desert, but the only white birds he saw were gulls, and they were not at all the same as the harbinger of Skywater with its ethereal length of neck, beak, legs, and trailing plumage.

The little fishing fleet from Santa Clara fanned out across the sea, and in its wake came a flight of brown pelicans. Like Chieko, Brand X was appalled to see boats with spirit-catching nets gliding across Skywater, but he noticed that at least the flanged trails the boats left behind on the water, unlike wide black trails on land, smoothed out and slowly vanished, leaving no trace upon the water.

He observed with great interest the pelicans following the boats. On the wing they were as imposing and significant-looking as hawks. The tips of their long, arched wings skimmed so close to the water they seemed to nick it. As he traced their glides and dives, he suddenly realized they must be hunting. It had never occurred to him there might be food in Skywater. He wondered what the food of spirits and of these big, brown birds with the scooping mouths might be and if perhaps the two-leggeds with the nets were dragging the water not for the spirits of moon-callers but for food for themselves. Could there be weeds and flowers, bushes and trees growing in the water? And living beings to be hunted and eaten?

All at once he pictured the fish fossil on his rocky outcropping, and he now remembered that during his greeting ritual along the shoreline he had caught an intriguing, vaguely hunger-arousing scent but had not stopped to investigate it. He stood, shook the sand from his fur, and, with a glance of invitation to Chieko, headed up the beach at his jerky, injured trot.

When he reached the pile of tangled kelp, he pawed and nosed aside its slick, bulbous, viny strands. Their rubbery texture was unpleasant to him, but he persisted in shoving them aside because he was certain of what he would uncover. When the dead fish was revealed, Brand X recognized it as indeed being a fleshed version of the fish fossil; but the flat gaze it returned with the big roundness of its wide open eye startled him. He gingerly tapped it twice with the side of his paw to be sure it was dead and lowered his nose to it carefully and slowly until it almost touched, then jerked it back as if fearing the fish might do something sudden, unexpected.

Chieko wagged her tail reassuringly. She had by now eaten several such washed-ashore fish. Although they were filled with many bones as tiny, clear, curved, and sharp as the claws of newborn pups, she had come to quite like their meat.

Brand X studied the fish lying rigidly in the sand. Its appearance seemed to him a composite of features from several beings he was familiar with. Its scaly skin had the glossiness of a snake's new skin as it emerged from the papery sluff of the old one. The shape of the fish's tail reminded him of a cactus wren's, and its fins of a dragonfly's wings.

He turned the fish over with his paw, flipping it out of its recessed outline in the wet sand. The side of the fish that had been down was coated with sand, the eye blinded by it. Ignoring the fish itself, he looked instead at the shape of the phantom fish lightly imprinted in the sand; it was more reminiscent to him of the fish fossil than was the fish itself.

He cocked his leg over the sand-fish shape and passed

water on it, then stepped back and looked at the mottles now marring the smoothness of its imprint and blotching its blunt outline. He remembered the way the stone-fish, when similarly wetted, had become vivid, not slurred, its every bone and fin more graphically revealed. He raked the outline of the fish once with his paw and was further disheartened to see four furrows gouged through it. The stone-boned fish had not changed when he scraped it with his paw.

As he looked at the sand-fish's furrowed, ephemeral, crude outline, he was overcome by longing not only to see the stone-boned fish again but to be sitting beside it on his rocky outcropping on the mountainside, looking out on the prickly, parched land which, despite its shortages, had always managed to feed and water him. From there, the world spread all around had always looked best of all to him, and whenever he had looked at the stone fish or given voice to his reverence for its ancestral home, his spirit had felt large. He now understood it was not thirst that had compelled his journey to Skywater. It was wanting to be where his spirit could always feel large within him.

Looking down at the sand-coated fish lying beside its meager, ruined imprint, he realized that he had not completed his journey after all. He had only finished the first leg of it. The completion of it would be when he arrived back at its starting point, the rocky outcropping with the stone fish.

Although no water-place on his home ground would ever be as fine and long-lived as the water tank of the old two-leggeds had been, the quick hard rains would come, as they always had, and fill the scooped-out catch basins and hollows in rocks and boulders and lie in wait underground for the paws of thirsty moon-callers to dig down to. And, after all, he reminded himself, even in the tall, white, wind-forged sand of the dunes there had been water.

His destination set, he rolled ceremoniously on the dead fish, and Chieko, too, took a turn. Kicking the sky, eyes vivid with elation, they scrubbed themselves back and forth on it, and their fur became gloriously infused with the rich scent of Skywater.

EPILOGUE

*But
don't worry about Coyote.
Being Coyote,
he lived.*

BYRD BAYLOR, *Moon Song*

From his rocky outcropping, Brand X looked down the mountainside at Chieko working her way up with labored slowness. The surge of energy that had carried him there had come of knowing they were almost at their journey's end. She lacked that incentive; she had never seen the stone imprinted with the bones of the Skywater being.

Now she never would. The fish fossil was gone. Its absence was a greater shock to Brand X than the undrinkable brine of Skywater had been. He swayed in abject incredulity over the hole that bore the shape of the rock's rough-edged, chunky underside and sniffed desperately at its rim. He was too lethargic with hunger, despair, gunshot pain, and exhaustion to care that a scorpion with its stinger curled over its back was scurrying around in the hole as if still disoriented by the light brought glaring down upon it by the stone's removal.

To spare Chieko the climb made futile by the fossil's disappearance, Brand X started back down the slope, his

bruised paws trying to avoid the small, sharp stones encrust-
ing the surface. When she saw him disconsolately picking his
way down toward her, she stopped and looked up at him with
the lackluster, depleted eyes of a refugee who has run out of
places to go.

Catching a scent, he halted and lifted his head. Chieko
watched to see where his nose was pointing, not caring what
he was smelling but only trying to gauge how much farther it
might mean she had to go.

He began to follow the aerial scent trail, and she followed
him as he slowly worked his way across the saguaro-strewn
mountain at the midway height where craggy, bare rock
jutted from the mountain's conical overskirt. The scent trail
led them to a stony eyrie projecting from the mountain like a
little balcony. A barrel cactus grew askew between its
gnarled, grayish brown rocks, and a young saguaro thrust itself up through a paloverde's nursemaiding branches.
Deeper beneath the paloverde and bolt upright as the
saguaro, stood a singular, slender slab of rust-red sandstone
weeping with black streaks.

Painstakingly selected by Albert Ryder, the desert-
varnished, triptych-shaped sandstone slab was the headstone
of Hallie Durham Ryder's grave. Albert had situated her
grave so that her head lay in the paloverde's shade and her
feet were toward the tip of the small, rocky promontory. The
rocks he had mounded atop the grave were his prize
specimens, the ones collected over the years which he had
been unwilling to sell. The topmost layer of the burial
mound contained geodes the size of cannonballs which he
had split into hemispheres so that their jagged, crystalline
centers would sparkle brilliantly when caught, as now, by the
first, eager light of the rising sun.

Burying her had nearly killed him. Indignant at her sug-
gestion of scrap pile lumber, he had made the coffin of iron-

wood. He had had to improvise a rig to pulley it, log by log, up the mountain to the place he had chosen for her burial site, and build the coffin on the spot. There were also the rocks for the mound and the headstone slab that had had to be gotten up the mountain. And Hallie herself. But as he had said when waving off her offer of help with the gunnysack of droppings that had spelled the end of happy times, it wasn't the weight of it. It was the *notion* of it. His thumbnail was still purple from the hammer blows that had missed when, blinded by tears, he had nailed her log coffin shut.

It was Albert Ryder's particular, cinnamony scent which Brand X had detected. When he and Chieko came upon him, he was sitting on the ground, wedged in the space between the headstone and the dazzling burial mound. Using the headstone as a backrest, he had his arms folded on his bent knees and his head down on his arms. He had just been overcome by a fresh batch of tears—old man's tears, unashamed as a baby's—when he felt eyes on him.

Raising his head very slowly, Albert wiped his nose on his shirtsleeve and swiped the crook of his elbow across his eyes. Without turning his head, he looked sidelong to see what was watching him. The two coyotes he saw standing skittishly broadside to him with their heads turned toward him, watching him intently, were so close he glimpsed the black whisker pores freckling their creamy muzzle stripes.

Recognizing them, remembering them, he felt such an upsurge of gladness at their return that his eyes prickled with tears, tears that felt different from the ones he shed for Hallie; these were not for whom he had lost but for who had come back.

"Well, well," Albert said softly. "Look who's here, a couple of my old drinking buddies."

Careful to keep his every movement slow and measured, he eased himself upright against the highest part of the staggered headstone. He kept his empty hands in plain view and his eyes lowered, knowing that if he returned their gaze he would spook them, making them act on their innate fear of him which, for the moment, was outweighed by something even more powerful.

He wished he could exchange straight-on looks with them. Not being able to look directly at them made it hard not to. Loneliness, that's what did it, he thought, loneliness for Hallie making him want a pair of smart eyes to talk to.

"Where have you two been all this time? I hope the others aren't far behind, old Dinty Moore and the rest of 'em. Just look at you! Sorriest-looking excuse for coyotes I ever saw! You sure are a sight for sore eyes though.

"And you, sir, what've you been up to to get shot at, huh? Well, lucky it was a shoulder and not your head. That name Hallie gave you suits you to a T. Brand X! She was real pleased with herself, coming up with that name for you."

Albert suddenly noticed that his tone of voice sounded just like Hallie's, as if, at her death, she had passed it on to him like a legacy: her talking-to-the-critters voice. He had always been too gruffly shy—even with his baby son—to take that fondly offhand tone, but it had snagged at his heart to overhear Hallie carrying on her comfortably one-sided conversations with Pete and, later on, the desert critters.

"I see you finally got yourself a lady friend there. Can't remember *her* name for the life of me though. Hallie'd know. She always was better at recollecting your names than I was. Where's that bossy sister of yours? Hoo boy, I remember her! She took after your mother in the way of meanness. Yeah, between your mama and your sister, you had a real tough row to hoe, little lady. But here you are, Brand X's missus, so I guess things come out all right for you in the long run."

Albert kept his head down as he slid his hand from his knee

up to his shirt pocket, took out a cinnamon ball, untwisted the cellophane wrapper, and slowly raised his hand to his mouth. Under the limp, turned-down brim of his battered sailor hat, Albert glanced over sidelong at Brand X and Chieko just to be sure they were still there, that they hadn't slipped off and left him talking to thin air.

"Looks like you've fared a whole lot better than Brand X there. *Him,* he looks like he ain't had a square meal since day one. But, wait a minute now, this is March. Maybe you're too full of pups to show just how skinny you really are. Yeah, bet that's it. How about that! She gonna make you a proud papa pretty soon, old timer?

"Well, whatever you two come for, it wasn't to pay your last respects to Hallie or watch an old fool blubber. I just like to come up here at daybreak to sit with Hallie a while and watch her birds for her. This always was her favorite sit-down spot. Now the sun's up I'll be going. It sure is good to see you again. I hope you're back to stay. I just wish Hallie knew you'd come back. Well, maybe she does."

He reached down and picked up a pair of mother-of-pearl opera glasses lying on the ground beside him. Brand X and Chieko, their eyes quickening, jerked skittishly at the sight of them.

"Now don't be scared. These prissy things couldn't hurt a flea. Hallie's mama brought them with her on the Chisholm Trail when she first come out to Kansas. I always meant to get Hallie some real field glasses for watching her birds with, even though she said she didn't want any. Said they'd make her feel like a peeping tom.

"I guess those field glasses I never got her and her never seeing an ocean are the two things I feel worst about. Born in the prairie, died in the desert. Landlocked all her born days. Not that she held it against me, our never making it to the coast, but I always felt like she was owed it, seeing something that big and blue spread out on top of the land like a bumpy picnic tablecloth. I sure wish I could give her an IOU for the ocean the same way she left me one saying she was sorry she had to die."

Too choked up to speak, he batted his hand flimsily at the air, drew up his knees to his chest, clasped his arms around them, dropped his head, and, his shoulders jerking, wept. His tears rolled off his cheeks, down between his knees and onto the rocks.

"The moon, it was puny the night she died, so the stars was just as clear as wet paw prints on a flat rock. I was sitting on my car-seat sofa there in the breezeway, and she called out from her trailer in that half-mad tone of voice she took with me. 'Albert Ryder!' she says. 'Come *here!*'

"Well, I didn't think nothing in particular about it, so I took my own time coming just to prove I wasn't at her beck and call. By the time I got there—I swear it couldn't of been more than half a minute though—she was already gone. Had the impatient look fixed on her Maker she'd had all set for me. Just as if to say, 'I called You. Now where *are* You?'

"I don't know what day of the week it truly was, but God Almighty, it sure was a Wednesday for me. It's a good thing she stuck on that P.S. telling me not to bury her in that old red-polka-dotted dress of hers, because I would of, thinking that after the sorrows that dress had seen it was about as funeral-like as any black one would of been.

"I took and burned that dress the day after she died. I did. Burned it! Cremated it! And then I hauled off and started kicking the ashes of it to the four winds, like it was all that dress's fault our boy got killed and the water got poisoned and she had passed away, but all of a sudden it seemed like I was kicking some part of Hallie herself, and I had to stop. Maybe there's a limit to *things* same as there is to people, and that dress had reached the limit of the grief that had gotten foisted off onto it. I saved them, the ashes of that dress, what was left of them anyway. Scooped them up and put them in a Folger's can. I keep them right beside my sofa. And I ain't ashamed to tell you I talk to them sometimes, too."

Albert sat up straight and fisted the tears off his cheeks, as if defying Brand X and Chieko to mock him for talking to the ashes of a faded red-polka-dotted dress. But, seeing they only listened and did not judge him, he lowered his head again.

"Anyhow, that's why I put this old fish fossil here by her headstone. Just to give her something that come from a real ocean, kind of like a little souvenir from where she never got to go."

Albert's head jerked up.

"God Almighty! Don't tell me! Is that it? Did you go up there where I dug it up from and find it gone and track me here? I bet that's it all right. There's nothing I wouldn't put past your kind in the way of smarts! Yeah, right there where this fossil come from was where you had your particular perch. Hallie and me could look up there most any sunset, and there you'd be, lying under that crooked old paloverde next to this fossil rock.

"I didn't mean to of stolen something you thought was rightfully yours, but, believe you me, I knew about this rock long before *you* ever saw light of day. I let it be, because I just liked knowing it was up there, maybe the same way you did. There never was any reason to disturb it till Hallie passed away and I wanted her to have it.

"I'm gonna get up now and go on down there to the shack. And if it *is* this old fish rock you came about, well, you're welcome to come and pass the time here same as I do. Hallie would be glad of your company. She always was real partial to you."

With one hand on the ground and one on his knee, Albert pushed himself into a crouch and straightened up slowly, not to keep from scaring off Brand X and Chieko but because it was the only way, at his brittle age, that he could get up. They backed up warily but did not bolt. He started off down the slope then turned half around.

"Tell you what," he said. "Hallie sure would of hated to see you two looking so wobbly and pitiful. Vultures'll carry you off if you don't get some grub right quick. I'll go see what I can dig up down at the shack, just this once, to help you get your strength built back up some."

Brand X waited until Albert was at the bottom of the mountain before approaching the fossil-bearing rock. It was imbedded almost flush with the ground in the narrow corridor where Albert had sat between the red sandstone slab and the crystalline-glittering burial mound. Shellacked by Albert's tears, the braille of the stone bones shone vividly. Brand X lowered his nose and sniffed the fish. Chieko hovered over his shoulder. He tentatively licked the wet, feathery-boned skeleton. He recoiled in shock, his eyes ablaze with reckless wonder. On his tongue lay the briny taste of Skywater, spirit water.

Albert Ryder slouched down on the car seat on the palm-thatched breezeway between his shack and Hallie's trailer. He stretched out his legs, crossed his feet, and rolled the cinnamon ball over to his cheek to make it easier to talk to Brand X and his missus whose name still hadn't come to him. They were warily stalking the metal water tank out by the mesquite and keeping a sharp eye on him.

"Well, go on," he said. "It ain't poisoned. Can't blame you for being suspicious though. I've seen plenty enough coyote bait that *was* doctored up with poison. Thought maybe you'd like it better if I set those pans in the tank, just for old times' sake.

"Atta girl, now you're getting the hang of it. Been so long since you ate good you almost forgot how. Never thought I'd live to see the day I'd be feeding and watering coyotes, but, shoot, I guess there's worse things than a little kindness. Hallie sure would of gotten a kick out of this. Bottled water and four big cans of beef stew!

"Well, it quiets down *my* Hallie Durham Ryder some. Guess your kind isn't troubled with one of those conscience contraptions. Thinking about Hallie never seeing an ocean and me never getting her those field glasses makes me wish I wasn't either.

"Atta boy, wash it down with some water. It sure is good to have a couple of my old drinking buddies back. Seems like old times, seeing a couple of you critters leaning in at the tank there.

"You got those bowls licked clean now? Thank you kindly, little lady, for that bit of tail-wagging you're doing. I surely do appreciate it. Well, you go on back up there to your old spot now. You'll be wanting to lie up for the day, specially the missus there. What're you looking at me like that for? Go on now. Scoot! Don't worry none about me. Just sing me a song or two tonight. Don't get me wrong, I ain't asking you to sing for your supper. That was my free of charge welcome-home to you."

Well fed and without thirst, Brand X and Chieko trotted up and slightly across the coyote-colored ground of the mountain's lower slope. Every so often they stopped to turn their heads in wonderment toward Albert, hobbling out into the harsh sunlight to fetch their empty bowls from the water tank.

As soon as they reached the wind-bent paloverde on the rocky outcropping, Brand X pawed the ground to loosen small stones and nosed them into the hole the fish fossil had left. When the hole was completely filled, he shut his eyes and threw back his head, offering his throat to the desert sky which the sun had claimed as its own, and he sent the proclamation of his return ululating out into the air. Chieko joined her voice to his, and their combined song was like a fragrance wafting throughout the valley.

Afterward, Brand X and Chieko lay down in the sun-stippled shade of the crooked old paloverde. Side by side, chests and heads high, ears forward, and spirits big, they surveyed the world that looked best of all from right there.

MELINDA WORTH POPHAM was born in Kansas City, Missouri, in 1944, and received a B.A. degree from the University of Chicago and an M.A. degree in creative writing from Stanford University. In the 1970s she worked as a foreign correspondent, and now lives in Malibu, California, with her husband and two children. *Skywater* is her second published novel.

The book was designed by Tree Swenson.
The type is Imprint, set by The Typeworks.
Manufactured by Edwards Brothers.